Reflections on Restoration

by

Rev Joe Kurian

SCOG Media Publishers
9 Norwood Road
Southall, Middx
UB2 4EA
copyright ©2015 scogmedia publishers
020 8574 6415
www.southallcog.com

First Published: October 2015
Printed in UK

About the Author

Rev Dr.Joe Kurian is the Director of the Church of God UK Cross Cultural Ministries and the Senior Pastor of the Southall Church of God in the West London area. Born and raised in Kerala, South India as the son of a minister and the grandson of a pioneer of the Pentecostal movement in South India, he devoted for the Christian ministry at the age of 18. Joe has attended the Mount Zion Bible College, Mulakuzha, Kerala and earned a Diploma in Bible. Along with his wife Simone, they were trained in Bible College in Katoomba, Australia and the Garden City School of Ministries in Brisbane, Australia where he was awarded a second Diploma and the Bachelor of Ministries in the early 1980's. Further on Joe and Simone attended the Pentecostal Theological Seminary and the Lee University respectively, in Cleveland, Tennessee, USA where he has earned the Master of Arts in Church Ministries.

In appreciation to his engagement and ministry of church planting among the cross cultural communities in United Kingdom and Europe, the European Theological Seminary in Ireland honoured him with a Doctor of Divinity. As an Ordained Bishop with the Church of God (Cleveland, Tenn.) he continues to engage in various ministries in Europe and around the world including speaking in various conferences, organising churches, training church leaders, mentoring future church workers, teaching and training in the local churches, supervising multi ethnic congregations, and "building bridges and breaking barriers" so that the Kingdom of God may expand and the Great Commission of Christ become a reality. Joe and Simone are blessed with three children (Phoebe, Timothy and Rachel -who along with their spouses love the Lord and support the ministry) and two grandchildren (Isabella and Domenico).

Preface

There is a sincere longing for restoration in the depth of all human hearts from the beginning of human history. The conscious awareness and feeling of inadequacy of not being able to be what man is created for, has been an issue that tormented humanity everywhere. Even with all the luxuries of life, man is still searching for significance and restoration.

The Holy Bible declares that "All have sinned and fall short of the glory of God" (Romans 3:23). Man, in his original state of creation was perfect in all aspects relationally, emotionally, spiritually, socially and was in harmony and fellowship with the Lord God. However, sin has separated man from God Who is Holy and Righteous. Adam and Eve chose to obey Satan and rebel against the Word of God. Since then man is distanced from God, corrupted in his thinking and stands under judgement and condemnation.

Nevertheless, man is not without hope, since the God of the Bible is a God of restoration. He wants to reinstate, renew, repair, rebuild and mend the mankind that has lost the God-given glory and reinvest the treasurers of heavenly riches in each one. He has made a way for man to return to Him and be restored to all that he has lost through Jessu Christ, our Saviour!

"Reflections on Restoration" is a series of short devotional thoughts on various aspects of Restoration, as discovered in the pages of the Holy Scriptures. I wrote these as the Spirit of God has lead me through the Word in my meditation. May the Spirit of God use these words on the printed pages to bring restoration and recovery to many souls that are still longing and struggling for meaning and restoration in their lives?

I would like to express my sincere gratitude and appreciation to the editorial team of the UK Cross Cultural Ministries in the shaping and publishing of this book. Recognition is made to Bro Dennis Chacko (Chair), Joel Thomas, Aman Verma, Sharon Salhothra and Lydia Salhothra. Special thanks and commendation to my dear wife and ministry partner, Simone. Also our three children (Phoebe, Timothy/Marsha & Rachel/Malcom) and our two grandchildren (Isabella and Domenico).
Be Restored!

Joe Kurian

Rev Joe Kurian
London UK

Contents

1. A SEASON OF RESTORATION

As we launch out to each day, with mixed feelings and expectations, we are reminded of God's promises, presence and his love and care throughout the year and beyond. in the scripture from Deutronomy 31:8 (ESV) we read "It is the Lord who goes before you. He will be with you; He will not leave you or forsake you. Do not fear or be dismayed." We declare this year a Season of Restoration! Yes, we serve a God Who is able to restore all that has been taken away from us by the enemy.

1. What is Restoration in Biblical Terms?

The secular dictionary states restoration as restitution of something taken away or lost; a return of something to a former, original, normal, or unimpaired condition; a putting back in to a former position or dignity. However, the Scriptures give us a different and superior meaning. When something is restored in the Scriptures, it always grows, multiplies or improves, so that its final condition is superior to its original state. (Job 42:10-12).

God restored Job after the terrible proofs which he was submitted, He gave him double that which he had lost and blessed more abundantly in his final days than at the beginning of his life. Jesus told His disciples that everyone who left something to follow Him would receive 100 times more. (Mark 10:29, 30)

God multiplies when He restores. He makes it grow, improve and become superior to the original state of the person/church. God wishes to make it more powerful, glorious and majestic, like nothing the world has ever seen.

2. Why should there be a Restoration?

a. God's Dignity Demands it.

The Almighty, Creator, Owner, Lord and King Who is Perfect, Holy, Righteous cannot put up with imperfection, decay, ruin, disrepair and shabbiness. The Creation in its origin was without any fault and "God saw that it was good" (Genesis 1:10) at the end of each day's creation.

The lost must be found! The broken must be healed! The distant ones must be brought home! The divided must be united! The wounded and hurt must be made whole! The contaminated must be cleansed! The twisted must be straightened! The bound and oppressed must be released!

b. Man's Depravity desperately needed it.

Apostle Paul wrote in Romans Chapter 3 and explains the total helplessness of man who stands guilty before a Holy God. Both Greeks and Jews (all mankind) are under the judgment and condemnation of God and is fallen morally, spiritually, socially and physically. (Romans 3:9-23).

But God Who is rich in mercy has designed a restoration program whereby the sinful, condemned man is able to stand redeemed, justified and sanctified before Him through the work of Jesus Christ on the cross. (Romans 3:24; 5:1; 6:22)

During this Season of Restoration, may we begin examining and listing the loss we suffered over the years. Whether we have lost the blessings and favours of God through the enemy's interruption or our own neglect, we must get into the process of restoration. It is a promise from our Father! It is provided for all His children! It requires steps of personal repentance and humility. Are You Ready for Restoration In God?

2. RESTORING SELF ESTEEM

It is the Season of Restoration! God is the Restorer of all that is irreparable, damaged, diminished, and destroyed and beyond human impossibilities. We as a church, family and we are about to witness the mighty move of the Holy Spirit through Whom unbelievable miracles and manifestations will take place to restore men women, families and the losses we suffered over the years!

1. Self-esteem

It is the self-worth sense of worth, confidence and self-respect of a person. It relates to your self-identity. Real Self-esteem is the value you place upon yourself as a person. Self-esteem is how you feel about yourself in the chambers of your mind. It is how you feel when you are alone in a crowd. Man is originally created with dignity, honour, self-worth, wholeness and in perfect union and fellowship with God Almighty. The Bible says, "Then God said, 'Let Us make man in Our image, according to Our likeness' So God created man in His own image; He created him in the image of God; He created them male and female . . . God saw all that He had made, and it was very good." (Genesis 1:26-27, 31)

2. Low Self-esteem

It is the feeling, or belief system of a person, that he/she is not good enough. A person with a low self esteem would feel very uncomfortable to face the real world, always feeling low, unworthy, and feels "good for nothing"! The low self-esteem comes from negative conclusions we draw about ourselves. Distortion is the thief that robs you of self-esteem. It is a destructive and unhealthy inferiority feeling of him/her due to childhood experiences and other external pressures and circumstances. Many Christians have developed a low self-esteem of "a worm as I am" thinking, though they bear the image of God in them through the work of grace in Christ. The consequences of low-self esteem are never ending and it has stolen the divine destiny, dignity and purposes of men and women on earth and beyond.

3. Hope and a Restoration

Could a man/woman, boy or girl who is affected and damaged by low esteem be restored to the healthy self esteem? Or is it too late for a person who has lived in a condition of lack of self respect and a sense of worth? There are several examples of real life stories of Bible characters who were suffering from this destructive emotional disease. Moses (Exodus 3:8-11; 4:10-17), Gideon (Judges 6:12, 15; Jeremiah 1:6), Amos (Amos 7:14) and Elijah are some of the mighty men of God who were very negative about themselves and rejected the call of God. They felt inadequate for the solemn duties God had called them to and promised to equip them to. There is hope and restoration for all who desire and yield themselves to the agency and power of the Holy Spirit.

Restoration of self-esteem, like any other rebuilding, relocating, re establishing, renovating exercise, requires a process where the person of low self worth discovers the foundational truth of human life and its purpose in the light of God's Word.

4. Overcoming Low Self Esteem

Three Basic Truths that helps raise our self-esteem are:

a. **God created us**

(Genesis 1:26-27) I am somebody, because I am created in the image and likeness of God Almighty. I am special, and not just another human being, because I have been fearfully and wonderfully made by my Creator. (Psalm 139:13-17) I am so special that my self-esteem depends on my Maker and designer.

b. **God loves us**

(John 3:16; Romans 5:6-10) God loves me unconditionally, unreservedly and allowed me to be as I am even when I did not know Him, did not honour Him and did not thank Him. As unworthy as I am, the thought of a loving God sending His only Son Jesus to bear my sin and die in my place, it is too much for me to believe and accept. Yet this is the fact! It raises my self -worth!!

c. **God chose us**

(1 Peter 2:9-10; Galatians 1:15-16) My feeling of rejection is not counted or recognised by peers, family and friends. Loneliness and other destructive thoughts are baseless as I discover that I am a chosen one for a special task and a mission to accomplish. Thank God for my healthy self-esteem.

3. STEPS TO RESTORATION

(Acts 3:19-21)
Restoration is a process that may require effort and time and a positive outlook. God Who is the Restorer has recommended some basic steps to be taken by all who desire to be restored and rewarded. The Scriptures are filled with sound teachings, warnings and spiritual guidance for the restoration to be completed in man and the universe.

Luke, the Physician wrote in the book of Acts of the Apostles, "Repent therefore and be converted, that your sins may be blotted out, so that times of refreshing may come from the presence of the Lord; and that He may send Jesus Christ, who was preached to you before, whom heaven must receive until the times of restoration of all things, which God has spoken by the mouth of all His holy prophets since the world began." Those who had taken backward steps in the past and distance from God and His purposes, must take forward steps to be fully reinstated.

1. Repent

No restoration is possible without true repentance. What is "repentance?" It is not just being sorry for the wrong we have done or said. Nor is it just a feeling of guilt. True repentance is reflected in a person by his change of heart, life and has a positive attitude whereby he/she is sorry enough to walk away from sin (quit sin) and walk towards the Giver of Life and be restored in Christ. It is 180 degree change, a complete turnaround from death to life.

Repentance is not a onetime event, but a continuous practice by a believer in Christ. Each time we repent of our short comings, draw backs, back sliding, sinful attitudes and practices and confess to God, we are being restored one step further. The number of steps that we went down from the truth of God must be climbed up in the process of restoration.

2. Renew

Restoration brings a person or a thing to its original condition for the primary purpose. A man or woman who has truly repented of their sins must be renewed in their spirit and mind. The sin stained soul and spirit requires a renewal by the Holy Spirit (Titus 3:5) to be conformed to the image of God. God's restoration plan is for the renewal of all that is contaminated by Satan and his demonic forces of evil (Ephesians 2:1-2). A renewal (revamp, renovate, repair, making it good) takes time and effort and steps must be followed to reach the expected goal.

3. Repeat
(Jeremiah 18:1-4) Is there hope for a marred vessel?
Could the same lump of clay be used by the potter to make another vessel? The Word of God teaches us that the God of Restoration is a God of second chance and many chances, if you didn't make it at the first chance.

God is like the potter who has the clay in His hands, and repeatedly make and reshape the vessels as it seems good to Him. The work of restoration has not finished in you as yet. It is being repeated by the Master Potter, our Creator God Himself.

Let us prepare ourselves, and take steps for restoration. Repent of our sins, be renewed in our spirits, and let God repeat the process in each one of us. Do not let go! Restoration takes time and effort. Stay in the hands of God. He will restore your favours.

4. RESTORATION OF JOY

"Restore to me the joy of Your salvation. And uphold me by Your generous Spirit" (Psalm 51:12) Have you ever noticed people who have lost interest in life altogether. No motivation or enthusiasm to achieve anything. Such people may laugh and express moments of courage, happiness and hope but seems to be short lived feelings and actions. Life goes through many experiences of interruptions and an unhealthy spirit has taken control of many people. These symptoms are clear evidences of the lack of joy in life.

Can the lost joy be restored in me? Will I ever be able to live a life that is full of joy, peace and contentment? What causes me to lose the joy? How can I be restored and be a person of joy and fulfilment in life? Psalm 51 gives us the reasons for the loss of joy and also the restoration process to former joy.

1. Reasons for the Loss of Joy

David was a man after God's own heart, but there were seasons he lost the joy and became troubled in spirit, emotions and body. Let us observe at least four reasons that he mentions that took away the joy from his life:

a.   Sin. (Psalm 51:1-4) David uses three different words to explain the sin he has committed against Bathsheba/against God Himself. "Transgression" means stepping over, breaking in, contravention, breach, infringement. "Iniquity" means wickedness, vice, injustice. "Evil" means immorality and wickedness. Sin steals the joy of a person. Those who indulge in sin cannot live with joy and peace.

b.   Uncleanness (Psalm 51:10) Sin contaminates the soul and spirit of man, the innermost being of a person is stained with sin and is declared unclean. So long as the person lives the stain filled life, joy goes out. David felt filthy before a Holy and Righteous God.

c.   Unsteady Spirit (Psalm51:10) Shaky, wobbly, wavering spirit in a man cannot contain the joy. Joy is permanent when the heart is settled and still, free from sin and uncleanness. The indwelling of the Holy Spirit helps a believer to keep his human spirit steady and healthy.

d.   Guilt (Psalm 51:14) Sin brings not only uncleanness and distance from holiness, but also shame and unhappiness. A guilty person shows it on his face, actions, voice, speech and by other behaviours. Adam and Eve wanted to hide, blame each other and cover up. Guilt took away the joy from David, so does it from all those who are driven by it. Guilt causes deep pain in the human soul and spirit.

2. Restoring the Joy

The lost treasure must be found, replaced, and restored to its former place and glory for the owner to be fully content. What are the steps one must take to be restored to the joy?

a.   Recognise (v.3). This means to be aware of, identify, and to know the sin that took away your joy. Discern the facts that have tampered with the inner peace, joy and contentment in life and keep such intrusions far away from you.

You need to have the courage to name the sin and do not "chocolate coat" and call it a sweet weakness! Acknowledging the sin is the first step towards restoration of the joy of the Lord.

b.   Confess (v. 4). This is not saying something to a man in a box. Confession means, to admit, to own up, to plead guilty, acknowledge, declare, and come clean. It is simply "saying just as it is". David's confession was to the Creator: "Against You, You, only have I sinned, and done this evil in Your sight". He said that he is guilty and he takes ownership to the evil and the immoral behaviour.

c.   Cleansing. (v.7,10) Sin's stains cannot be removed by good works or religious ceremonies. The cleansing is only by divine agency as we yield our mind, soul and spirit to the Holy Spirit. David prayed, "Purge me, And Wash Me". What a relief and feeling of ease when the stains of sins are washed away by the blood of Jesus and the Word of God.

Your joy can only be restored when you discover the reasons and take steps for **Restoration!**

5. THREE ASPECTS OF RESTORATION

The God of the Bible is a God of restoration. His love drives Him consistently to seek and search for the lost, lonely and the last. In God's eyes nothing is irreparable, no one is hidden or unreachable, and nothing remains "under the carpet". He is a Restorer of all that seems beyond human possibilities. Each and every lost ones must be found and restored.

The Gospel of Luke Chapter 15 records the three parables of Jesus. It is a "Chapter of Lost and Found." Jesus used parables to teach people deeper spiritual, moral and ethical truths. His method is still one of the best in teaching and preaching techniques. It starts from the known to the unknown, from the familiar to the unfamiliar, from earthly to heavenly, from natural to supernatural.

What can we learn from these parables of Christ about Restoration?

1. **Restoration to Safety** (Luke 15:4-7)- The shepherd who had a flock of one hundred sheep has lost one. He goes in search of it, finds it and brings back to the fold and rejoices for the rescue and recovery. The sheep was lost to its security, comfort, provision and protection when it is strayed and outside of the limits of the shepherd's sight. There is no safety outside of the will of God. So long as Adam and Eve were within the boundary of God's instructions (Word) and will, there was safety and security. But when they chose to step out from the comfort and plan of God and wander off to the sound of strange voice, danger was around.

But God is still following after the "lost sheep"; humanity that has lost in sin and the dangers and consequences of it- and to restore them to safety and salvation in Christ. Let us pray with the Psalmist, "I have gone astray like a lost sheep; seek your servant..." (Psalm 119:176; Luke 19:10; John 10:1-18) The Good Shepherd restores the soul into safety.

2. **Restoration of Value** (Luke 15:8-10)- A woman has lost one of the ten coins she had, then she lights a lamp, sweep the house and searches for it until she finds it. The coin is lost to its usefulness when it is not found in the hands of its owner. Its value is not recognised and made use of as long as it remains lost and under the carpet.

There are many useful and valuable "human coins" that are lost to their worth, usefulness, potential and honour due to the condition In which they are in now. These "coins" will only be useful and valuable when they are found and brought back to the place/Person (God) where they will be fully used to their maximum potential. Do you feel like a lost coin? Lost in the house, unrecognised, unnoticed, never made to use for the purpose you are created for? The Restorer values you and is seeking to raise you up and bring you to full potential for His glory.

3. **Restoration of Identity** (Luke 15:11-24)- The younger son (prodigal) of the father leaves home with his possessions, wanders off to a far country, wastes all his wealth, lost his dignity, honour, position ,privileges and promises of a comfortable life with the father's blessing!

He was so lost that he did what he did without any sense. A loss of common sense led him to a riotous living which has eaten away his wealth, dignity and identity.

When he came to his senses he realised how far he is from the father's house and how much he was missing the company of his father and the favours he used to enjoy. He decided to return to the father's house. His father recognised him from far and ran to him and embraced and welcomed the lost son back to the house.

This is the true picture of restoration into full son- ship with all the privileges. God's restoration program is likewise, and He brings back the lost and broken ones and reinstate them with dignity and honour.

Dear brothers and sisters, if you feel a loss in any areas of your life, the Restorer is ready to re-establish you. Come to Christ just as you are, with your losses, brokenness, pains, traumas, troubles and miseries, He will restore you.

6. RESTORATION OF LOVE

"Nevertheless, I have this against you, that you have left your first love."- Jesus (Revelation 2:4)

How can the virtue of genuine love be lost or left? What causes people to be less serious and careless when it comes to the expression of authentic and unconditional love? Is there hope for those who are left behind, betrayed, taken advantage of in the name of "love"? Can the lost/left love and the parties that have neglected be restored?

The Book of Revelation Chapters 2 and 3 records seven messages to seven churches of Asia Minor in the early Church period. These messages are spoken by the risen Lord Jesus Christ, and are commendations, warnings, rebuke and directions to churches.

The Church of Ephesus (Revelation 2:1-7) is known as the "loveless church". Among the many good qualities, Jesus mentioned a serious and deliberate mistake of the church: "that you have left your first love". It was not lost, but they left. It seems that the church was too busy and diligent in the church work, that they left the work of the Lord Jesus, and failed to nurture the personal intimacy with the Master. Isn't this the condition of many churches and Christians of today?

First love is pure

Pure love has no hidden agenda or any reservation. It is the love that has the 1 Corinthians Chapter Thirteen qualities. The Ephesian Christians knew and experienced the love of Christ, when they first believed the Gospel and became born again and Spirit-filled followers of Christ. God loved us first, even while we were still sinners (Romans 5:8). We responded to God's love by obeying and serving Him and humanity in His love. Our first love for Christ must never lose or leave its flavour, passion and intensity.

Many have left the first zeal, enthusiasm, drive and motivation to follow the Lord due to various other reasons. Some have let the worldliness and its pleasures to take over their life's purpose, and to enjoy the temporary gratification. Others have traded in for intellectualism and modernity instead of remaining in the first love. Few others have adopted a different Jesus and "another gospel"; a Jesus who would say yes to the demands of the human flesh and ego; a gospel that promotes prosperity above righteousness and holiness!

Restoration of your love that has gone cold will take place when you:

1.   **"Remember** (Revelation 2:5) from where you have fallen". Go back to the memory lane and put yourself in the hands of Jesus. See where you were without Christ. And remember His grace and mercy through which He has saved you and brought you this far!

2.   **"Repent** (Revelation 2:5) and do the first works". Restoration of the first love is complete only when true Godly sorrow that leads a person to recognise the condition. Duty without devotion is not genuine. A heart of repentance will go back and do the first works with the first love.

7. RESTORATION OF FAITH

"Now faith is the substance of things hoped for, the evidence of things not seen" (Hebrews 12:1). God cannot be known or experienced without faith. (Hebrews 11:6) Yet even among the so called believers and followers of Christ, there seems to be a lack or loss of this essential ingredient and quality. I believe we all need to be alert and awakened to this reality and take steps to be restored in our faith and faithfulness to God and the things of God. A casual faith is not good enough.

Reasons for Loss/Lack of Faith:

1. **Lack of Understanding** - Knowledge is power. Knowing Who God is and what His purposes are for life would create a deep hunger and trust in the human hearts. When you know that faith is the medium by which you can approach God, there will be a natural drive to exercise trust in Him. (Philippians 3:8-11; 1 Timothy 1:3-7; John17:3; Hebrews 2:1-4). Ignorance and deliberate rejection of the knowledge and the purposes of God is a   hindrance and will block the human hearts and minds to grow in faith. If your foundation is not solid what you build upon will eventually collapse.

2. **Lack of Exercise** - When we stop exercising, our muscles grow weak and the body feels it. Faith that is not stretched and used regularly is also the same. The more we put our God-given faith at work to develop, to grow deeper and stronger in relationship with the Lord, the more it advances in maturity. Use it or lose it! (Hebrews 3:12-19; Mark 2:1-5; 16:17-18; Hebrews   Chapter 11 – the Chapter of Exercised Faith). When was the last time you have stretched your faith, even to the point of "breaking" and God responded to your sincere faith?

3. **Lack of Obedience to the Word** - (Romans 1:5) Faith grows in the rich soil of the Word and prayer. Faith is generated by the hearing of the Word (Romans 10:17) and it only works when it is followed by the unquestioning, unhesitating and wholehearted obedience to the demands of the Word. "By faith Abraham obeyed when he was called to go to the place which he would receive as an inheritance" (Hebrews 11:8). When your faith is not mixed with obedience and exercise, it begins to lose its strength and eventually becomes a weak and an inactive faith. Let us take God at His Word and watch what He does in response to your genuine faith and obedience to the Word of God!

4. **Lack of sincere practical Christian living** - (1 Timothy 1:19-20). The Apostle Paul reminds and warns Timothy of some people who have rejected the purity and sincerity in the faith. " .. Having faith and a good conscience, which some having rejected concerning the faith have suffered shipwreck." It is easy for anyone to believe in Christ. But it is entirely a different matter to behave what you believe. A good and genuine believer will have a clear conscience to live a practical Christian life based on the teachings of the Lord Jesus Christ. Hypocrisy will affect the strength and power of your faith. You will lose the vitality and purpose of faith.

"Lord I believe, help my unbelief" (Mark 9:24) prayed the father of the boy possessed by deaf and dumb spirit. Restoration of our weakened, casual, and stagnant faith is possible by repentance, renewal, obedience, exercise, education and by daily drawing closer to the Author and Finisher of our faith, Christ Himself (Hebrews 12:2).

8. RENEWAL BEFORE RESTORATION

The restoration of anything requires effort and it is often through a process. God is not in a hurry and He has been patient with the rebellious, distant and disobedient children. He restores the broken relationships and spirituality by allowing people to take steps of renewal.

The Book of Haggai speaks of the restoration process of the people of God who had returned from the Babylonian captivity. The rebuilding of the temple in Jerusalem was a priority for the returnees. But it seems that after the initial enthusiasm and commitment, the people have lost the passion to pursue the building project. Their personal affairs interfered with God's business and the community as a whole felt the consequences that affected their lives.

What areas in their lives needed renewal?

1. **A Renewal of Passion–** The urge, the appetite, the craving for the completion of the building of God's temple was not evident in the people when Haggai met them. Instead the passion was diverted for selfish gain, and a greed for personal possessions. We must prioritise the Kingdom business first "and all these things shall be added unto you". (Matthew 6:33). Where is your passion today?

2. **A Renewal of Courage–** A big project like the rebuilding of the destroyed temple demands a great amount of courage in the Lord. Restoration is impossible without the united and courageous effort of the people who are assigned to the work. Fear and frustration is the enemy of any forward looking and progressive project. How bold and courageous are you to rebuild the broken down relationships?

3. **A Renewal of Holiness–** Haggai spoke with boldness and convinced the priests that the people are contaminated and have lost the holiness that is expected by God. Restoration is a distant dream while people indulge in sin and compromise the truths of God. Unholy hands cannot build a holy temple and expect the Holy One of Israel to meet them and be among them. "Sanctify yourselves" says the Lord.

4. **A Renewal of Faith–** God is in control of the future and He can be trusted in all circumstances and at all times. A huge task of restoration requires a great faith that is renewed. When God said, "From this day I will bless you" (Haggai 2:19), the people were expected to wholeheartedly trust Him and keep working on the project. Does your faith need a faith lift/face lift?

Haggai speaks to us today with the same tone and focus. Restoration is followed by Renewal. It is personal renewal and congregational renewal. Are you ready for it? The God of restoration will fulfil what He has promised. But the people are expected to renew and recommit to restoration.

9. RESTORATION OF HOLINESS

What do we mean by holiness? Is it something we in the 21st Century, should be concerned about? Shouldn't we be more focusing on personal development, a health and wealth prosperity oriented gospel proclamation and accommodating the variety of contemporary expressions of worship and spiritual exercise? Or does the Bible say otherwise?

It seems that the church of today is too much into self-gratification, group-justification and celebrity glorification and has forgotten the core values and principles of life as written in the Holy Bible. Holiness is a foundational teaching and expected life style of all followers of Christ, regardless of their distinct identity and doctrinal/cultural orientation. Sadly, we do not hear many sermons and exhortations from the pulpits now a days. But the Word of God cannot be compromised or altered and it still stands for the standard of holiness.

The Church of God, from its inception, is a "holiness movement" which has an article in its Declaration of Faith (Article7) "We believe Holiness to be God's standard of living for His people."

Why do we emphasize the standard of Holiness?

a.   **God is Holy**- "Ye shall be holy, for I the Lord your God am holy". (Leviticus 19:2) We serve a God Who is glorious in holiness and does not compromise with un holiness and the works of darkness. Even heaven is not found clean and holy before the fiery eyes of God (Job 15:15). It is God's nature and He just cannot be something else, but to be holy all eternity. Jesus the express image of God in human form lived a holy and pure life and it is attested by His friends and enemies alike.(Hebrews 7:26).

b.   **God's Restored People are holy**- ".. that you put on the new man which was created according to God, in true righteousness and holiness." (Ephesians 4:20-24) The original creation of man in the "image and likeness of God" was marred by the influence of Satan upon Adam and Eve. That which was lost or disfigured, stained or spoiled by Satan is restored in the newness of man when he/she is "born again" by the Spirit of God (John 3:3,5) and by the Word of God (1 Peter 1:23). Every believer who is born again and indwelt by the Spirit of God is expected to grow in holiness and righteousness. (1 Thessalonians 5:23)

c.   **Without Holiness?**- (Hebrews 12:14; Revelation 22:11,15) The Scriptures are clear and declared throughout the Old and the New Testaments that without holiness one cannot see God! Our faith and practice as Christians should reflect God's standard of holiness always. We have no substitute for a holiness living. Church attendance, charitable works, religious observances, trying to discipline our habits are not substitute for the sanctifying work of the Holy Spirit.

Heaven is prepared only for sanctified people, who are forgiven by Christ upon their faith in the sacrificial work of Christ on the cross; who are consistently obedient to the Word of God and growing in to the image and likeness of Jesus Christ. May you be a sanctified believer and growing daily in pursuit of His image.

10. FROM DESTRUCTION TO RESTORATION

Jesus said, "The thief does not come except to steal, and to kill and to destroy." (John 10:10). From the beginning of human history it was the intention of Satan to disrupt and destroy the plan and purpose of God for mankind. That which the enemy has started in the Garden of Eden, continues and has spread to all peoples everywhere. "All have sinned and come short of the glory of God" wrote the Apostle Paul. (Romans 3:23)

However, God has prepared a plan of restoration for all creation. The Bible records the heart of God for man's redemption and restoration. Jesus the Son of God, became Son of Man to rescue and restore mankind from eternal destruction.

The Gospel of Mark Chapter 5 is a Chapter of Restoration from Destruction. Let us examine this Scripture portion and see the miracle of restoration by Christ:

• Verses 1- 20 **The Restoration of mind** (dignity, honour) - healing of the demon possessed man in Gadara.
• Verses 21-24; 35-43 **The Restoration of life** – raising of Jairus' daughter from death
• Verses 25-34 **The Restoration of health** – healing of the woman with the issue of blood

May I encourage you to take some time and carefully read the Chapter and observe the destructive conditions that existed in these three people. Also discover the process of restoration.

1. Destructive Conditions:

• **The demon possessed man** has lost his right mind due to demons controlling and directing him to engage in destructive things. He was possessed of an unclean spirit, dwelling in dangerous places, violent behaviour, untameable, crying out and cutting himself with stones.

• **The daughter of Jairus** was severely sick and at the point of death.By the time Jesus came to the house of Jairus preparations were made for the funeral of the young girl. Too late for anyone to do anything humanly possible. The hope of the family and friends were destroyed by the untimely death.

• **The woman with the issue of blood**. Lost her health, wealth, and lost trust in the medical professionals, about to lose her life if condition persists. Ceremonially unclean, and mentally withdrawn due to the pressure of the society.

2. Process of Restoration

The total restoration is the work of the restorer, our Maker and Saviour. However, He works through a process where the divine power and the human co-operation come together.

The demon possessed man was not in a condition to believe and act upon the Word of God. But Jesus spoke to the powers that controlled him and said, "Come out of the man, unclean spirit." (Mark 5:8) The words of Jesus penetrated through and beyond the grips, strong control and possession of the legions of demons in the man." It (the Word) shall not come back to Me empty..." (Isaiah 55:11). He was sitting and clothed and in his right mind (verse 15). Let us use the authority and power in the Word to restore the ones who lost sanity.

Jairus was a religious leader who confessed the person and power of Christ. He said to Jesus, " My little daughter lies at the point of death. Come and lay Your hands on her, that she may be healed, and she will live." (Mark 5:23) Restoration requires a confession of faith in the Restorer. Only the Author of life can offer life back to the one who has lost it. Nothing is too late for the One Who is in control of all situation, including death. At the commanding words of Jesus, the little girl who was dead, arose and walked. (Mark 5:41-42)

The woman with the issue of blood had to press through the crowd. Her faith in the Person of Jesus and the power He has over everything has driven her to act upon and touch Jesus' clothes "If I may touch His clothes, I shall be made well" (Mark 5:28-29). Her restoration was instant, and the flow of blood dried up. Move on with the condition but with the promise and your faith in Christ who makes all things new.

11. RESTORATION: THE MISSION OF THE PASSION

We remember the passion of Jesus Christ, just before He went to the cross.The crucifixion, burial and resurrection of Christ is the central event of redemption of mankind from their sins and curse. The ultimate purpose of the passion of Jesus is with the divine mission of rescuing the man from eternal death. By the death of the One and Only Son of God, many sons may be brought to glory.(Hebrews 2:10)

The Mess– Mankind is in a messed up, disorderly and chaotic state since Adam and Eve chose to rebel against God and His perfect purpose. Distancing from the way of righteousness and pursuing the path of flesh and finding shortcuts to gratify the desires of the flesh led man to all kinds of problems and issues. Man is lost, became short of the glory of God, darkened in his mind and understanding and utterly helpless to return to his original state.The mess still continues in men and women everywhere in the world. (Romans 3:23).

The Message– God saw the mess and the helpless state in which man is entangled for generations. However, immediately after the Fall of man God spoke a message that has eternal consequences for those who are willing and obedient to receive and abide by it. In Genesis 3:15, we read about the message of the Seed of woman, who will bruise the head of the serpent and that His heel will be bruised by the serpent. This is the first prophetic message that the Messiah will be born as the seed of the woman and will come with a mission of rescue and restoration.(Galatians 4:4)

The Man– Restoration of mankind is possible only by a Super Man, who shares the nature of the lost man (Psalm 49:7-9; Hebrews 2: 9,10, 14-18). Paul the apostle wrote about this Supernatural Being (Christ) who put on the form of man to identify with humanity. (Philippians 2:5-8). He writes to Timothy about this Man, "For there is one God and one Mediator between God and men, the Man Christ Jesus."(1 Timothy 2:5). The song writer Graham Kendrik put it this way, "Meekness and majesty, Manhood and Deity, In perfect harmony, The Man who is God, Lord of eternity Dwells in humanity, Kneels in humility And washes our feet." This is your God!

The Mission– John 3:16 spells out the mission of the passion. "For God so loved the world that he gave His only begotten Son that whoever believes in Him should not perish, but have eternal life. "Restoration was 'mission impossible,' but the incarnation (God coming in the flesh and dwelling among us - John 1:14) opened the way for the initiation of the mission to the lost humanity. "And the Lord has laid on Him the iniquity of us all" says Isaiah prophetically about the transfer of our sins upon the Lamb of God. (Isaiah 53:6).

The Cross was not a tragedy

 It was a triumph over sin, death, and the dire consequences that brought to humanity. When Jesus died on the cross, while giving up His Spirit, he uttered these words, "It is finished." (John19:30). Mission accomplished. Christ has crossed over the gulf that was made by sin. His pain was for our gain! " He was wounded for our transgressions, and He was bruised for our iniquities". Jesus paid it all! The Mission of Passion was Restoration! May we offer praise and thanks to our Saviour who went to the cross and did it for us, once for all! Hallelujah. Even in the grave He is Lord!

12. RESTORING THE REDEEMED

"Brothers, if someone is caught in a sin, you who are spiritual should restore him gently." (Galatians 6:1)

God's restoration is extended to all people everywhere, regardless of their status and the gravity of their offense. The community of believers (the church) is called to be agents of restoration and be actively engaged in turning people back to the right path.

Does a believer in Christ need restoration? Isn't he/she already been forgiven and that their names are in the Book of the Lamb? Do they need a further restoration? The Word of God is clear in this matter: "all have sinned and come short of the glory of God" (Romans 3:23). Also that, it is possible for a Christian to fall into sin, to back slide, to become spiritually ineffective, short sighted and be distanced from the power and productivity of the Spirit of God.

1.**God's Desire for Restoration**- Everything that has lost its position, privilege and pre-eminence must be brought back to its original condition. Then only the work of restoration is complete. The fallen man stands guilty and condemned before a Holy and Righteous God. From the beginning, God has initiated the restoration process to bring the fallen man back to his original state and glory.

A Christian who is caught up in sin and had fallen from the grace is also in the plan of God to be restored. (James 5:19, 20). There is no sin too dark that the blood of Jesus cannot wash away, as the sinner/saint repents of them and asks for the mercy of God. (1 John 1:6-10). God wants all His prodigal sons and daughters to return to Him and enjoy the full fellowship.

2. **God's Design for Restoration**- God uses the redeemed ones on earth as His agents to carry out the process of restoration. Paul wrote to the Galatian Christians, "..If a man is overtaken in any trespass, you who are spiritual restore such a one in a spirit of gentleness.." (Galatians 6:1) It is divinely designed to draw the distant ones by those who are physically present and spiritually sympathetic to the ones who have caused the offense.

The work of restoration must be done in a spirit of gentleness. Here the Scripture does not give the brother or sister in Christ the power or right to condemn, criticise, or expel the offender, but to offer him the love and compassion and a non-judgemental acceptance with the intention to restore him/her. Only a truly restored redeemed Christian is able to enter in to a process of restoration as designed by God.

3.**God's Delight in Restoration**- The shepherd who found and brought the lost sheep back to the fold; (Luke 15:4-7) the woman who had lost a coin and found it after searching carefully (Luke 15:8-10); the father whose son went out and wasted his wealth and life, and later saw him coming back to the home (Luke 15:11-24), all these three have expressed their joy when the restoration took place. Their joy had no limits and greater joy was in heaven when a sinner repents and accepts Christ as the Saviour. The writer of Hebrews declares God's Word, "But if anyone draws back, My soul has no pleasure in him." (Hebrews 10:38).

If you are a redeemed Christian, there is a solemn responsibility and privilege bestowed upon you to restore the wandering Christians and those who are caught up in sinful habits. Listen to the words of James the Apostle, "Brethren, if anyone among you wanders from the truth and someone turns him back, let him know that he who turns a sinner from the error of his way will save a soul from death and cover a multitude of sins." (James 5:19,20).

May we be non-judgemental and offer guidance and support for the wandering believers who are caught up in sin and entangled. Let each of us become instruments in God's mighty hands to bring restoration to the needy. The Lord delights in you as you serve Him.

13. RESPONSIBLE RESTORATION

Isaiah 58:12, "Your people will rebuild the ancient ruins and will raise up the age-old foundations; you will be called Repairer of Broken Walls, Restorer of Streets with Dwellings."

Restoration is a process with partnership and responsibility. Though God is ultimately the source and strength behind every restoration, human partnership and serious responsibility is expected for the completion of the task.

Let us examine the prophetical promise of God through Isaiah and discover the efforts and extent of the restoration plan of God for people and places.

1. **Restoration begins with the Return of the exiles**- If God allows an exit from Israel, He is able to bring them back with a promise. However, the people must respond in faith and trust, and take steps to return to the land of their fathers in order to fulfil God's purposes. Under the leadership of Ezra, Nehemiah and Zerubbabel many of the exiles in Babylon have returned and began to work to restore the glory of their heritage. If we have walked out of the plan and purpose of God and failed to fulfil the responsibilities he has placed upon us, it is time to return to that spiritual heritage. Each of us must listen to the voice of God and the promptings of the Holy Spirit and return to the promises of God. "Remember therefore, from where you have fallen; repent and do the first works..." (Revelation 2:5)

2. **Restored people are Responsible for Rebuilding**- The Babylonians have destroyed the temple of God in Jerusalem and have destroyed the identity of the Jewish nation. Through God's mercy those who were taken captives are offered freedom to return and rebuild the wall, temple and the nation's identity. Men like Nehemiah, Ezra and Zerubbabel played a big part in the restoration of the people and their spirituality. The apostle Paul said to the Christians in Galatia, "..you who are spiritual restore such a one in a spirit of gentleness.."(Revelation 6:1). It is the responsibility of every believer in Christ, to reach out to the broken, battered ,shattered and crushed lives and raise up and rebuild.

3. **Restored People will be remembered for their Responsibility**- Isaiah wrote that those who are instrumental in the work of restoration will be honoured and remembered. They will be called Repairer of Broken Walls, Restorer of Streets with Dwellings. (Isaiah 58:12). They are involved in Rebuilding and Raising Up. The work of restoration is not an easy task. It is a very responsible work that requires serious commitment and hard work. It is natural that at times we forget to give credit and honour to such men and women who have worked behind the scene to achieve a common goal. But God will never forget and will honour you with privileges not known to the world.

Dear brothers and sisters in Christ, do you take restoration seriously and responsibly in your life and in others? There are people who are distanced and are in "exile" in a foreign land and under the dominion of Satan. Let us launch out and restore them. Let us do it responsibly and remember, the Lord rewards all who are sincerely seeking for restoration of lives.

14. "WILL YOU RESTORE THE KINGDOM TO ISRAEL?"
(Acts 1:6)

A National Question

The disciples of Jesus asked this question that has to do with the restoration of Israel's status as a nation. They lost the rank and privilege as a kingdom by the fall of Southern Kingdom (Judah) being taken as captives to Babylon around B.C.600. When Jesus came and announced the Kingdom of God, it seems many people, including His own disciples failed to grasp the spiritual nature of God's ruler ship upon people. Therefore, they asked the risen Christ whether it is time for the nation of Israel to reclaim its sovereignty. The thought of restoration in all aspects of our lives is crucial. However, the process of restoration does not begin on a national scale. God's promise of restoration will be fulfilled in God's way and in His time.

A Personal Response

Jesus responded to the question of the disciples first of all, by reminding them of the divine prerogative and the supreme authority of the heavenly Father over such issues. Instead, He gave a personal response to the group of disciples that they will be given a power that surpasses the political kingdom of Israel. And that they will be witnesses of the Lord Jesus Christ with the power of the Holy Spirit. " But you shall receive power when the Holy Spirit has come upon you..." (Acts 1:8).

A national, political restoration was anticipated by the Jews at any cost by any leader due to the loss of power, dignity, racial identity and the preservation of future generations in Israel. But the divine order is that personal restoration must take place primarily (Acts 2:38-42), and then it will spread to the national and beyond the borders. We must pray and ask the Lord, "Will you restore me now?".

A Universal Scope

God's restoration program has already begun since the Fall of man in the Garden of Eden. The personal restoration has a universal scope. Restored people who are empowered by the Holy Spirit are driven beyond the national, racial, ethnic and geographical borders with the message of Christ. The disciples' question was mainly a local one, concerning Israel. But Jesus has empowered them and send them out with a worldwide vision and ministry of restoration. He said, "... and you shall be witnesses to Me in Jerusalem, and in all Judea and Samaria, and to the end of the earth." (Acts 1:8).

What a promise! What a Scope! God our Heavenly Father wants all His lost sons and daughters to be brought back to His Home. As much as He is concerned about the national, political restoration of Israel or any nation, He still is very much interested in personal restoration that leads to local, regional, national and universal reconciliation, restoration and revival.

15. NOT WELL AT JACOB'S WELL
(John 4:4-42)

The story of the Woman at the well is recorded only by the Gospel writer, John. In this account, Jesus is meeting a Samaritan woman, who did not have a good reputation in the city. However, the encounter with Christ has transformed the woman and she was able to experience real joy, meaning and restoration in her life.

Let us discover the state of the woman and the restoration offered by Christ our Saviour.

1.**She was at the Well, but was not well!**- Jacob's well was significant for the religious Jews. Biblical tradition and archaeology has proof enough of a well that was probably dug by Jacob to provide water for his family (Genesis 33:18-20).The woman had a bad moral character and life style, and is spiritually unfit. She was practicing co habitation (she had five former husbands and the one with whom she was living was not her husband!) She came to draw water from the well on her own due to her shameful habits and to be kept away from the public. We can be found at the source of water still be left thirsty, lonely, rejected and seeking approval.Jacob may have provided his children with physical water in an arid land, but Jesus provides His children with "living water" in a spiritual wasteland. The life Jesus gives satisfies all our needs and springs up to eternal life (John 4:14).

2.**She knew the religious history, but did not know His Story!**- In the conversation Jesus had with the woman, we notice that she had some knowledge of her heritage and background. She had mentioned of the racial discrimination between Jews and Samaritans (John 4:9), the greatness of father Jacob in her religious history (John 4:12); the places of worship, for Samaritans and the Jews (John 4:20). However, the woman was ignorant of the Messiah who was speaking to her all things (John 4:25). The story behind all history is His (Messiah's) story of coming to this world and seeking the lost. Boasting in one's traditions, achievements and heritage itself do not make a person justified, reconciled or restored before God.

3. **She knew the Place of worship, but missed the Person and the Power of true worship-** The woman said to Jesus, "Our fathers worshipped on this mountain, and you Jews say that in Jerusalem is the place where one ought to worship" (John 4:20). This woman must have known and practiced the external rituals and ceremonies in Samaria all her life, without knowing the true meaning of worship. But Jesus opened her understanding by revealing the essence of true worship, "the true worshippers will worship the Father in spirit and truth; for the Father is seeking such to worship Him. God is Spirit, and those who worship Him must worship in spirit and truth" (John 4: 23-24). At this point the woman confessed that the Messiah is coming and He will tell us all things. Then Jesus said to her that He is the Messiah.

The knowledge that Jesus Christ is the promised Messiah to come and restore everything, and that He was speaking to her, must have shocked the woman. That she left her water pot and ran into the city and told them: "Come and see a Man who told me all things that I ever did. Could this be the Christ?" (John 4:29). The whole city came and saw and believed and confessed that "this is indeed the Christ, the Saviour of the world."(John 4:42).

Well, now the woman can say, "It is well with my soul". A restored soul, refreshed by the Saviour and then reaching her own town and bringing them to the source of living water, and not to the well. Are you well? Or are you still at the well? Let the Saviour satisfy your inner thirst for the living water- life from Christ that springs up to everlasting life

16. RESTORING THE SOUND DOCTRINES

"For the time will come when they will not endure sound doctrine, but according to their own desires, because they have itching ears, they will heap up for themselves teachers; and they will turn their ears away from the truth, and be turned aside to fables." (2 Timothy 4:3,4)

There can be no practical Christian living, without systematically and consistently following the teachings (doctrines) passed onto us by Christ and His apostles. Although Christian life is not about following set rules and legalistically abiding with the principles laid out by the Church, doctrines play a great part in the foundation and advancement of Christian life and service. Disregarding the established doctrines of the Scriptures could result in a distorted Christianity.

Even from the first century, early apostolic church we notice the diversion from the true and sound doctrines. As a result of this the church had to face schisms and unwanted heresies that diverted people from the essence of true Christianity. A restoration of sound doctrines is an urgent need of the church of today.

What do we see in the New Testament and beyond?

1. **Apostolic Doctrines (Acts 2:42)**- "And they continued steadfastly in the apostle's doctrine and fellowship, in the breaking of bread, and in prayers." The teachings of Jesus Christ has been given initially to the apostles (Matthew 28:19-20) and they taught the early Christians to practice them as they follow and commit themselves to Christ and the community of believers. They included the basic and fundamental truths and practice of repentance, water, baptism, Holy Spirit baptism, separated (sanctified) life, breaking of bread (communion), fellowship and prayer (Acts 2:38-47). Anyone who joined the Church in those days were familiar with these doctrines and abided with it. All Christians of all ages are expected to follow these foundational and essential teachings and practice that are ordered by the Lord and the apostles.

2. **Additional Doctrines (Acts 15:5)**- The early church had its roots in Judaism, since Jesus our Saviour was born in a Jewish family and grew up with customs and traditions of the Jewish religion. The Christians who came from Judaism insisted that the newly converted gentiles be circumcised before they are full members. This was not part of the original apostolic, authentic teaching, but some insisted that they add this "burden and yoke" too. The apostles called a Council and discussed this matter and decreed that the additional burden should not be expected by anyone. It is the scheme of the enemy to belittle Christ and His authoritative teaching by adding unnecessary man-made traditions, customs and burdens.

3. **Altered Doctrines (Galatians1:9)**- We read about the perversion of the Gospel by some intruders who have hidden agendas within the faith community. Paul has addressed and warned the Galatian Christians about the alteration and perversion of the truth of the Gospel. It is the preaching of another gospel, than the true Gospel proclaimed by Jesus and His apostles. It was a gospel that brought bondage and slavery again for the person. Instead of justification by faith alone in Christ, they have altered it to observe the Law. Paul challenges them by asking,

"You ran well. Who hindered you from obeying the truth? (Galatians 5:7) Repentance is altered to penance, confession to a priest! Water Baptism by immersion for believers is changed to sprinkling of water on infants (Christening). The Biblical teaching of Christ's mediator- ship (1 Timothy 2:5) is changed to many human mediators, including dead "saints" and Mary the mother of Jesus!

A restoration of sound doctrines is important for sound Christian living and service. To believe wrong means to behave wrong. May we go back to the apostolic doctrines and live out apostolic Christianity and experience apostolic advancement in building God's Kingdom.

17. RESTORING TRUE WORSHIP

The fallen mankind is desperately in need of restoration in various aspects of his life. The first human beings were created by God with perfection and for a purpose. Man and God had such an intimate communion between them, that Adam and Eve could hear the sound of the Lord God walking in the Garden of Eden in the cool of the day. (Genesis 3:8). But man's choice of rebellion and sin has broken the true fellowship with God and he became fearful.

Man, by nature is a worshipper. However, the sinful man has lost the focus of true worship and has given himself into the desires and cravings of the flesh. "Although they knew God, they did not glorify Him as God and their foolish hearts were darkened." (Romans 1:21) The false worship began to appear when man "changed the glory of the incorruptible God into an image made like corruptible man and birds and four footed animals and creeping things." (Romans 1:23).

God has manifested His true identity and power throughout human history and have raised up men and women to restore true worship in His chosen people. In the First Book of Kings, Chapter 18, we read about Elijah's effort to restore true worship in Israel. He has been successful in turning the people from the pagan God of Baal, and destroy the forces that stood against the true worship of Jehovah.

Let us learn some steps in restoration lead by Elijah:

1. **Elijah Re assembled the people (1 Kings 18:30)**- People in Israel were scattered in their loyalty and worship due to the evil headship of the nation, King Ahab. Many have turned away from the Lord God and the true worship they had been taught and practiced for generations. There were divided loyalties and dis spirited prophets of Jehovah, hiding in the caves (1 Kings 18:13) for fear of Queen Jezebel, who had massacred many prophets of God. A re assembly was inevitable for the restoration. "Elijah said to all the people, "Come near to me"; so all the people came near to him." It is time that we as God's chosen people gather together and be under the anointed leadership of the servants of God.

2. **Elijah Repaired the Altar of the Lord (1 Kings 18:30)**- " .. And he repaired the altar of the Lord that was broken down." We cannot expect a restoration without a thorough repair of the broken down altars. Altar is the place of sacrifice, bloodshed, giving up, submission, and complete surrender. Where the stones of the altar is broken down and in disarray, it must be brought back to order and in shape. God cannot do a work of restoration or manifestation of His power, where the altar is altered according to human wisdom. Preparation at the altar is a pre-requisite for God's operation and manifestation. Where do we need a repair in our attitudes, spirituality and service?

3. **Elijah Responded to God in Prayer and Trust (1 Kings 18:36-37)**- The people are rallied together, the altar is rearranged and repaired, and now God is ready to act. Elijah prayed to God in full faith and trust, knowing that he is a faithful God. Two things were at threat here: God's reputation and Elijah's safety! The prayer was in response to God's proven record of trustworthiness and faithfulness (Lord God of Abraham, Isaac and Israel) and the confidence that He will answer the prayer at this critical time

Elijah's deepest desire was that the people's hearts will be turned back to the true and living God. That the true worship will be restored in Israel.

God is faithful to honour the sincere and simple, heart-felt prayers of His children and reveal His glory and restore the true worship. "Then the fire of the Lord fell..."(1 Kings 18:38). God Who answers by fire will also answer us in an age of backsliding, spiritual apathy, and religious Christianity.

Have you lost the true spirit of worship? Are you scattered, confused and following false Gods and ritual and hollow spirituality? If so, it is time to take steps like Elijah and challenge the false prophets of Baal in the authority and power of Christ our Saviour.

18. RESTORING God'S VESSEL

"Let the gold and silver articles of the house of God.be restored,..each to its place" (Ezra 6:5)

God specialises in bringing back the honour and value in the lost, displaced, and broken vessels. Regardless of the length of time, the kind of abuses and the conditions in which these vessels had been through, the mercy of God will restore them to its original place and honour.

The Book of Daniel begins with a narration of the invasion of Jerusalem by Nebuchadnezzar, the Babylonian king. The city and all its inhabitants were under his control. Many people of quality and skills were taken away along with some of the articles (vessels) of the house of God (Daniel 1:1-2). These vessels and articles were used in the temple in Jerusalem by the priests and high priests for holy purposes in worship and sacrifices unto Jehovah. Now they are displaced and are kept in the house of pagan God.

Let us have a closer look at these vessels: They were...

1. **Displaced Vessels**– They are moved from its place by external forces. The vessels knew their place and were content with the honour and dignity bestowed upon them. When they are removed and placed in a strange place and among unfamiliar surroundings, the vessels cannot settle. This happens to believers in Christ, when they are forcefully and at times by wrong motives and persuasion removed from where God has placed them.

2. **Distanced Vessels**–The distance between Jerusalem and ancient Babylon is approximately 500 miles. The vessels in the temple of God were closer to the priests and worshippers of Jehovah and were in the company of people who served a living God. Now the distance of place has brought difference in worship, language, culture, and rituals etc. which are not familiar to the vessels. When men and women distance themselves from the living God, and the spirit of worship and praise, they could end up in a far away country and far away from the presence, purpose and power of God.

3. **Desecrated Vessels**– The vessels in the house of God in Jerusalem had dignity and honour as long as it was in the house and used by the priests for the holy purposes. Now the Babylonian king had taken them and kept them in the temple of his God. Not only that King Belshazzar brought shame and stain to these holy vessels when he used them for a drunken party (Daniel 5:1-4). This can happen when we as God's chosen vessels, give ourselves into the hands of unGodly people and wrong company. Our worth and value is only identified by our use and purpose in the hands of God and in the house of God. Outside is shame, disgrace, desecration and death!

But there is hope for a vessel that is Displaced, Distanced or Desecrated. God's restoration is extended to all in spite of any damages caused by Satan, self or others.

After 70 years of captivity the captives are set free and were allowed to take back the articles (vessels) of the house of God with them back to Jerusalem. Under the leadership of Ezra,Nehemiah and Zerubbabel many Jews have returned to their home land and they built the wall around the city and rebuilt the temple that was destroyed by Nebuchadnezzar. The Persian King Darius issued a decree and Ezra records it in Chapter 6 of his book. In verse 5 we read, "And let the gold and silver articles of the house of God, which Nebuchadnezzar took from the temple which is in Jerusalem and brought to Babylon, be restored and taken back to the temple which is Jerusalem, each to its place; and deposit them in the house of God."

What an honour, and a jubilation when restoration takes place to the displaced, distant and degraded ones.

There is a rest in restoration, because you are settled in your rightful place.
There is a trust in restoration, because you are back to the temple and fulfilling the purpose of God. Dear brother, sister, friend are you like the vessels that were displaced, distanced and desecrated? If so do no waste any more time. Be restored, and be planted and be useful in the house of God.

19. THE RESPONSIBLE SHEPHERD

("He restores my soul" Psalm 23:3)
One of the most loved and memorised portions of the Scriptures is Psalm 23 - The Shepherd's Psalm. The Bible speaks of God as the Shepherd and the people as His sheep. Throughout the Old Testament Israel is pictured as the sheep in the fold where God is seen as the responsible shepherd caring and guiding the people. Jesus, our Saviour Himself has spoken many times in the Gospels and used parables to teach the relationship of the shepherd and the sheep.

What are certain responsibilities and duties of a true shepherd? Among the many, let us consider the following:

1. **He Recognises the sheep** (John10:14,27)- To recognise means, " to know, identify, be familiar with, distinguish, spot, make out, aware of" etc. Jesus said, "I know My sheep and am known by My own". A true shepherd can identify and distinguish each of his sheep and their nature and needs. The welfare of the sheep is dependent on the knowledge of the shepherd about each one in the fold. If you are a believer in and a follower of Christ, you are known by Him as an individual with distinct qualities, and He is able to meet your needs. You are not considered as a crowd, but counted as a distinct person.

2. **He Refreshes the sheep** (Psalm 23:1-2)- This is the rejuvenation, energising, re charging and the revival brought about by the nourishment. The sheep must be brought out to the pasture land for grazing and to the water bays for quenching the thirst. The believer is in need of daily feeding on the Word of God and being filled with the Holy Spirit to be renewed and refreshed in life and service to God. The shepherd is responsible to lead the sheep to the still waters and to the green grass.

3. **He Rescues the sheep** (Luke15:4-6)- It is to release, liberate, save, and set free from bondages and troubles. Sheep can easily go astray and be lost. (Psalm 119: 176;Luke 19:10) A responsible shepherd takes risks to rescue the sheep in danger. A sheep that has gone astray cannot by itself return to its fold. It needs to be searched for, found and brought back to the sheep pen. Jesus, the Good Shepherd is a responsible shepherd and has come to seek and to save us from our sins and curse. Now the Church is called to "rescue the perishing!"

4. **He Restores the sheep** (Psalm 23:4)- To restore means, to reinstate, re-establish, repair, bring back and renovate The sheep could fall sick, go astray, be snatched away/stolen by strangers. It's physical, mental and emotional stages could affect the health adversely due to the unexpected incidents and circumstances the sheep is found. However, a responsible shepherd will not waste any time, but make every effort to repair the damages and reinstate the affected sheep. He will bring it back to its original condition and offer security and value. If you are a lost, lonely, abused, distanced, defiled, damaged believer, the Restoring Shepherd, Jesus Christ is willing to reinstate you. Will you come to Him today?

20. RESTORATION OF SOUND DOCTRINE

"But as for you, speak the things which are proper for sound doctrine." (Titus 2:1)

The mark of a healthy church and a strong Christian is found in the Biblical foundational teachings and practical application of the New Testament, apostolic doctrines. The history of the Christian church shows that from its beginning there were unhealthy and doctrines of demons (1 Timothy 4:1) that were taught and spread among the church. The early Church Councils had to deal with many erroneous doctrines that were in contradiction with the teachings and practice of Christ and the first apostles.

The Church of today is warned to be extremely cautious of doctrines that are non-biblical and incompatible to the body of doctrines accepted and promoted by the early church. When wrong doctrines are promoted, we can expect wrong practices and a shallow Christianity. Let us take the following steps in restoring the true biblical doctrines for the New Testament Church.

1. **Recognise the Sound Doctrine-**. (Titus 1:9; 2:1; 2 Timothy 4:3). It means to know, distinguish and identify the true apostolic teachings and practices that were accepted by the first century Church of God. The opposite of sound doctrines means superficial and shallow teachings that may not require any sincere commitment from the believers. How do we recognise the sound doctrines?

The following Three test questions will help us to recognise the authentic New Testament teachings:

• **What did Christ say about it?**
• **What did the early apostles say about it?**
• **What does the early history of the Christian Church/ the Church Fathers say about it?**

2. **Reject the Shallow and Erroneous Doctrines-** (Galatians 1:6-9; 1 Timothy 4:7) Paul the apostle had to write to the churches and leaders of the first century Church to warn them of erroneous teachings that were creeping in the Church and instruct them to hold on to the sound doctrines. He warned Timothy of "deceiving spirits and doctrines of demons" (1 Timothy 4:1) and instructed him to "carefully follow the good doctrine" False and half-true doctrines are brought into Church by Satan in a subtle manner. It is presented as sounding good, but it is dangerous.

3. **Renew our Commitment to Sound Doctrines-** (1 Timothy 4:13) Among the many crucial instructions given to Timothy, the early Church leader, Paul the apostle had this emphatic word, "..give attention to reading, to exhortation, to doctrine" (1 Timothy 4:13). If we do not renew our commitment to the doctrines we will eventually lose the importance of practicing them. That which we fail to commit to will be omitted in due course. The first Church in Jerusalem was not only committed, but "they continued steadfastly in the apostle's doctrine and fellowship, in the breaking of bread and in prayers." (Acts 2:42). One of the qualities searched for and expected in a Church Leader (for e.g. Bishop or Elder) is that he should be "able to teach". God is a God of restoration. He is longing to see the Body of Christ restored in its doctrinal purity.

21. RESTORING THE NEW TESTAMENT DOCTRINES
The Value of Good Doctrines

The life and service of a Christian, and the Church as a Body of Christ is directed by the established teachings of the New Testament. The Church of God is built upon the doctrines that are taught by Jesus Christ and practiced and handed down to the Church universal by the early apostles and the church fathers. However, in the passing of two thousand years since Christ, we may find variations and strange practices that are incompatible to the core Biblical teachings.

Let us observe the following values of the Doctrines:

1. **Doctrine defines the devoted disciples** (Acts 2:42)- From the beginning of the Christian Church, we are told that there were believers who obeyed and practiced the apostolic and accepted teachings (doctrines). Luke the physician wrote in the Acts of the Apostles that those who received the Word that was preached to them on the Day of Pentecost were devoted to the leadership and the discipline of the community of faith. "And they continued steadfastly in the apostle's doctrine..." writes Luke. The test of their faith and their commitment to the body of Christ (the Church) was marked by their adherence to the doctrines taught by the apostles. Faith in and confession of Jesus Christ as the Lord and Saviour, and acceptance of the core values of Biblical standard as practiced by the early apostles defined a dedicated follower of Christ.

2. **Doctrine unites the different believers** (Ephesians 4:1-6)- Good doctrines that are grounded in the Word of God and are passed on to us by the early apostles bring unity in the body of Christ. Several of the New Testament epistles (letters) were written by Apostle Paul and others to correct and confront the unwholesome and divisive teachings brought in by false teachers in the first century. But the core teachings of the New Testament unites the Church, locally and universally. Paul the apostle wrote to the Church at Ephesus and persuaded them to "keep the unity of the Spirit in the bond of peace. There is one body and one Spirit, one Lord, one faith, one baptism, one God and Father of all..." These are uniting factors in the church as members from diverse backgrounds are grafted into the body of Christ.

3. **Doctrine establishes the dissident Christian** (Ephesians 4:14-16) The Church is a family, where members of different levels of maturity and understanding live together. There are some vulnerable "baby Christians", who are not established in the faith by the grounding of the Word and doctrine (1 Timothy 5:17; Hebrews 5:12-14). These young and unbalanced believers are the target of the false teachers who spread "wild and half true" doctrines that are not in line with the rest of the body of Scriptures. But the teaching and commitment to the good doctrines of the New Testament would establish the unsteady, non-conforming believer, who are "tossed to and fro and carried about with every wind of doctrine, by the trickery of men, in the cunning craftiness of deceitful plotting..". May the Lord restore the distant and dissident ones and establish in the apostolic doctrines. New Testament teachings that are taught by Christ, handed down and practiced by the apostles and early church fathers are the foundational doctrines upon which the Church of God stands. Let us restore the neglected teachings and practice (e.g. Baptism of the Holy Spirit with the initial evidence of tongues, sanctified life style, the standard of holiness) and revive the Church for the end time ministry.

39

22. RESTORING THE IMAGE OF God IN YOU

A person's value, worth, self-esteem and dignity is dependent upon the healthy image that is deeply ingrained from within him/herself. All of us are concerned and cautious about our looks and demeanour. Our image goes deeper than the external physical appearance and how we adorn and present ourselves before others. There are many people in our world with broken, damaged and faulty images who are searching for identity and true meaning of life. Man is desperately in need of a restoration and renewal into the original creation, Restoration of the Image of God!

1. Man bears God's Image (Genesis 1:26, 27)- The Bible tells us that man is a unique creation of God. "Then God said, Let Us make man in Our image, according to our likeness. So God created man in His own image; in the image of God He created him; male and female, He created them". (Genesis 1:26-27) This is the record of the original creation of the first man from whom all humanity traces their ancestry. This was a healthy and positive image since it had the fresh imprint of the Creator. This was not a physical image and likeness, but a spiritual, social, mental and moral likeness. Man reflected the purity and depths of God's image in all these aspects in his original creation. Man possessed a perfect image and a healthy outlook.

2. Satan ruined God's Image in Man (Genesis 3:1-24)- God's imprint and image in man has suffered damage due to sin and rebellion. Satan, the enemy of God and the image of imperfection and evil entered man's world and disrupted the close communion with God and the healthy image. Man is fallen from the perfection and is guilty and condemned. "All have sinned and come short of the glory of God" says Paul the apostle in Romans 3:23.Now man is left with a broken image that is stained and corrupted with sin. His entire being (body, soul and spirit) is affected and became destitute, expelled from the Garden of Eden and became a victim of separation, pain, hatred, violence, sickness and death. Man lost his originality, identity and the destiny with God in heaven.

3. Christ Restores the Image of God in Man (Hebrews 2:14-18)- Jesus Christ is "God became flesh and dwelt among us" (John 1:14). The purpose of God's incarnation (coming in the form of man) in Christ was to rescue and restore man from his lost and damaged image and give him new hope and eternal life. Christ died a substitutionary death for all mankind who came under condemnation (Colossians 2:13-15) and is risen from the dead to offer new life and blessed hope for all those who believe in His work on the cross.

Now you can have a restored image of God! Listen to the words of the Apostle Paul "... and be renewed in the spirit of your mind, and that you put on the new man which was created according to God in true righteousness and holiness." (Ephesians 4:23, 26). He wrote to the Colossians, "... put on the new man who is renewed in knowledge according to the image of Him who created him." (3: 10).To the Corinthians Paul wrote, "Therefore, if anyone is in Christ, he is a new creation; old things have passed away; behold, all things have become new". (2 Corinthians 5:17).

Be restored in the image of God as you receive Christ as your Saviour and make Him your Lord. " we shall be like Him, for we shall see Him as He is." Says John the beloved Apostle. (1 John 3:2). He will "transform our lowly body that it may be conformed to His glorious body..." (Philippians 3:21)

40

23. RESTORING THE GIFTS

God is the Greatest Giver ever, and the best Gift to mankind is Jesus Christ, the Saviour (John 3:16). The Word of God tells us about the various kinds of gifts given generously to mankind for life and service. However, in the passing of time and generations the God-given gifts are neglected, abused, and left undeveloped for the purpose they were given. The Giver of all good gifts is still desiring that men and women will be restored in their use/exercise of gifts.

The gifts that we all are blessed with are divine endowments for specific purposes and ultimately for the glory of God. Wasted gifts are a waste of God's precious resources that could have been used elsewhere by someone else. With the investment of gifts in man comes a great responsibility and accountability. We all must give an account to God for the talents we have been entrusted with.

In the process of restoring the God-given gifts in us, we must take note of the following:

1. Surrender your gifts (Romans 12:1-2)- Restoration of gifts and the full benefit of them begins with a total surrender of the life. Paul wrote to the believers in Rome and exhorted, " ..that you present your bodies a living sacrifice...". God can restore and use only that which is surrendered to Him. Boasting about our gifts or taking glory and pride in our service comes from a selfish heart. God cannot bless when self is exalted. Jesus must become the Lord of all our lives and gifts in order to be restored. " Therefore, humble yourselves under the mighty hand of God, that he may exalt you in due time"(1 Peter 5:6). Handing over the gifts to the Giver is the first step in restoration.

2. Serve with your gifts (Romans 12:3-8; 1 Peter 4:10,11)-
The New Testament list of gifts can be divided into three categories:
1) Motivational Gifts - (Romans 12:3-8)
2) Manifestation Gifts - (1 Corinthians 12: 7-10)
3) Ministry Gifts – (Ephesians 4:11.)

All these spiritual gifts are given (distributed to) among the believers for service to God and service to fellow human beings. Withholding or refraining from using the God-given talents, abilities and gifts results in the gifts being wasted and the service to needy people abandoned. Regular exercise sharpens the skills and brings health to the body. Likewise the service offered to the Body of Christ and the people at large brings restoration a reality. Unused gifts and talents gathers dust and shows signs of rust and erosion. Spiritual gifts and talents must be used wisely and regularly.

3. Stir up your gifts (2 Timothy 1:6)- Paul the Apostle challenged and encouraged young Timothy to "stir up" his gifts. It is to fan into flame and sharpen for more effectiveness. A dormant gift is equal to lifelessness, because it is inactive. Many are gifted, and even few are boxed. As long as the gift remains in the box/container and no one does anything about it and make use of it, it is wasted for ever. Therefore, Timothy is warned to stir up, to restore and re use the gifts. Christians are called and equipped by the Lord to engage in a dying world and draw people from their destruction and bring them to the Saviour. Let us stir up what we have and use it for His glory.

24. RESTORATION OF RELATIONSHIPS

The Bible is a book of relationships. Its main theme is to restore the broken, disengaged/detached and lost humanity back to the original perfect communion with the Creator. God, as the loving and reaching Heavenly Father has been working to reinstate the damaged relationships in His creation, since the Fall of Man.
The letter to Ephesians by the Apostle Paul is a classic document on the demonstration of the restoration in relationships. Let us examine the restorations of communion (harmony) in:

1. **God and Man** (Ephesians 2:1-10) This is the foundation of all other relationships. When the fallen man is reconnected with his Maker and restored in the image and likeness (spiritually) it prepares the ground for solid and sustained relationships in other aspects of his/her life. Jesus came to redeem, reconcile, renew and restore mankind.

2. **Jew and Gentile** (Ephesians 2:11-22)-Detachment from the Maker resulted in disconnection between mankind, race, nationality, ethnicity, language, and culture that began to divide and distance man from fellow men. The cross of Christ has broken down the middle wall of separation between the Jew and Gentile. A new humanity is created by bringing these two together in the Church, as they are, fitted and built together.

3. **Christian and fellow Members** (Ephesians 3:14-4:16)- Now the relationship is getting better as believers commune with each other under the Lordship of Jesus Christ. They are like members of one family, keeping the unity of the Spirit in the bond of peace, and complementing each other by the exercise of their gifts, and contributing in the growth and maturity of the Body of Christ.

4. **Husband and Wife** (Ephesians 5:21-33)- Here we see the restoration of a renewed covenant relationship between man and wife. That which Adam and Eve could not maintain in the Garden of Eden is restored in the new covenant in purity and love. "Submitting to one another in the fear of God" is the order. (Ephesians 5:21).

5. **Children and Parents** (Ephesians 6:1-4)- Restored relationship in the parents is passed on to the Godly generations after them. Our children are copy cats, and our demonstration of practical role model is a challenge to them. Obedience and submission are both taught and caught. Let there be no prodigal children in the family of God.

6. **Employee and Employer** (Ephesians 6:5-9)- We live in a world where many people are exploited of their privileges and rights.The relationship between masters and servants in Paul's days has a universal application and relevance to our contemporary culture. Paul's prescription in verses 5-9 of Chapter 6 gives us fundamental principles to follow and abide with for restored and healthy relationship.

Christ is the source of all restoration. The Holy Spirit, through the agency of the Church executes the work of restoration in man and in the community at large. It is an ongoing work and requires the cooperation and commitment of all believers. May we be instruments and channels of restoration for peace and harmony in a broken world?

25. RESTORING INTIMACY WITH God

Intimacy with God is seldom spoken now a days. It seems the need of in depth communion and fellowship with God is abandoned by the Church as a whole and many Christians. I believe we can hear an urgent call from the Holy Spirit that the Church must focus on a deeper and sustained intimacy with God. May we be revived in this much needed area of inner spiritual quality?

1. **The "Thieves" of Intimacy with God–** What or who takes away the desire of intimacy with God? We must catch the thieves and clear the path for intimacy to sustain. Let me mention the following "thieves" that hinders our intimate communion with our Saviour, Weariness, Laziness, Wandering mind (boredom), Busyness, Problems, Guilt, Worldliness, Unbelief, Fear; Hiding (guilt); Self-Esteem; Selfishness/Pride; Rejection; Bitterness/Resentment; Immaturity; Irresponsibility; Dishonesty; Devaluation; Addiction; Reactivity; Poor Priorities; Talkativeness; Control issues; Sin; and Unfaithful. Can you identify with any of these symptoms or attitudes/ behaviours in your own life? Catch the thieves that destroy your closeness and communion with the Father in heaven.

2. **Intimacy is initiated by God Himself** (Genesis Chapter 2)– From the creation of the first man (Adam & Eve), God desired to commune with man. Though fallen by man's sin and rebellion the Almighty God continues to seek and find ways to fellowship with man who bears the image and likeness of God. God begins and initiates that which is good, but sin and Satan spoils and disturbs the plan. Jesus, our Saviour has brought the highest intimacy possible for mankind on earth. " The Word became flesh and dwelt among us" (John 1:14).

3. **Intimacy is illustrated in human love & marriage**(Song of Songs Chapter 2; Ephesians 5: 22-33)– The purest and best form of human love is exhibited in the account of Song of Solomon, where the words and feelings of expressions between the lover and the beloved is mentioned. The climax of intimacy between a husband and wife is manifested in their pure and sanctified sexual intercourse. God expects that kind of depth in our fellowship and communion with Him. Our love and loyalty/ commitment to God must be deep and consistent, a love and intimacy that know no limits and dare to go extra miles in demonstrating them.

4. **Intimacy is cultivated in spiritual exercises–** God is a Spirit and we are made in His image and likeness. We are commanded to " love the Lord with all your heart, with all your soul, and with all your mind." (Matthew 22:37) No works of the flesh, or rituals and religious ceremonies can satisfy the longing of God's intimacy with man. God delights in the praises of His people and sincere, honest and heartfelt thanks giving and worship is accepted by Him. May we take time to deepen and restore our intimacy with God by the following: prayer, scripture reading, worship, fasting, witnessing, obedience to the Spirit's guidance, fellowship, engaging in practical service to the community.

Have you lost the intimacy with Jesus, due to interruptions and instances that happened in your life? Isn't it time that you worked on restoring the intimacy with Him? Will you take necessary steps and be restored? Jesus is coming for His bride, who is intimately in love with Him. Many will be sadly left out. Get right and be restored in your intimacy with God.

26. RESTORING THE ZEAL FOR THE REALITY

What is meant by having the zeal or being zealous? To have zeal means to be a person full of enthusiasm, passion, fervour, keenness and eagerness. Our God is passionate about His mission and the man he created to fulfil His mission. He has never lost the zeal, and is always at work in restoring broken men and damaged relationships. What about you dear brother/sister and friend?

There are various kinds and degrees of zeal mentioned in the Word of God. It is for our admonition and caution and to be zealous for the right purpose. Let us discover few as we search the Scriptures:

1. **Zeal without Knowledge** (Romans 10:2)- Paul made reference to the religious, orthodox Jews of his time, saying, "that they have a zeal for God, but not according to the knowledge." Among the Jewish sects, Pharisees were the most fervent, and at times fanatical people as far as their religious faith and observance is concerned. They have a misplaced zeal because it is not mixed with knowledge and reality. May we be zealous in all matters provided we are grounded in reality?

2. **Zeal for the Traditions** (Galatians 1:14)-The Apostle Paul being a religious Jew with strict Pharisaic traditions, upbringing and education was showing his zeal and passion in them. This zeal has provoked him to resist the Way of Salvation through Christ and destroy the people of the Way. Good traditions that enrich and empower us in the faith are beneficial. However, when any tradition prevents and restrains us from moving on to the revelation of the Scriptures and the Person of Christ we must take a break from it and obey God than our traditions.

3. **Zeal of Generosity** (2 Corinthians 9:2)- " .. and your zeal has stirred up the majority." Christians in Corinth are commended for their enthusiasm and eagerness in the spirit of giving generously to those who are in need. This is zeal for reality as they exhibit generosity. This kind of zeal is commendable because it is contagious, and it causes the community to have the zeal that moves them to action.

4. **Zeal of Ministry/Service**- "Never be lacking in zeal, but keep your spiritual fervour, serving the Lord."(Romans 12:11).Spiritual gifts and graces are granted to believers for sacrificial and sincere service. What God has invested in us must be put to use in the best possible ways and with the highest degree of zeal and fervency in our spirits. We cannot afford to lag or be laid back but move forward with the passion and the power of the Holy Spirit in us. Luke the historian, Physician and Gospel writer mentions Apollos as a "man (who) had been instructed in the way of the Lord; and being fervent in the spirit, he spoke and taught accurately the things of the Lord.." (Acts 18:25). This was a minister with zeal.

Churches and believers are called upon to restore their zeal and passion in a generation of cold spirituality. Jesus quoted the verse from Psalm 69:9, "Because zeal for your house eaten me up." Let us catch the zeal and purpose of our Saviour. It is time to restore our passion for reality. Are you ready?

27. RESTORING THE PURPOSE OF THE CHURCH

The Church as the Body of Christ is established for a purpose. Jesus, the Head of the Church has given clear plan and specific purpose for His followers as they function as the "salt" and "light" of this world. The early apostolic church had clear direction and uncompromising commitment to the mission of Christ. But the Church of 21st century has distanced far from its original purpose and drifted towards the tides of today.

1. **What is the Primary Purpose of the Church?**- Many people have various perceptions and preferred opinions about what the Church should do or be like. But our understanding and affirmation of the purpose and the existence of the Church should be from the Word of God. The Head of the Church, Christ, has the final   authority in declaring the clear purpose of the Body of Christ.

The Church exists for the purpose of representing the Lord Jesus Christ and in reaching, teaching, and making disciples of all nations. It is called the Great Commission (Matthew 28:19,20). The Great CO-mission is a GO-mission and is an O-mission if not taken seriously by the Church.

2. **How Can the Church Be Restored to its Purpose?**-The Church as a body must take urgent and serious steps to get back to the original intended purpose given by its Head, the Lord Jesus Christ. The New Testament books are the source documents we can depend upon for our guidance in the process of restoration. The following are certain priorities and practices the Church must return to re discover its primary purpose- exalt christ, edify the body and evangelise the world.

- Worship, Fellowship, Discipleship, Stewardship, Evangelism, Prayer and such spiritual exercises brings the Church closer to its Lord.
- Knowing the heartbeat of Christ through prayer and fasting, meditation on the Scriptures, hearing the voice of the Spirit and seeing the needs and feeling the hurts of the broken world alerts us to the purpose of our lives as followers of Christ.
- The Church must take a U turn and go back to the Upper Room and experience another "Pentecost" to be restored to its original purpose..

3. **Characteristics of a Restored Church**- Paul's letter to Ephesians give certain characteristics of a purpose driven Church.

Ephesians Chapter 1 - It is an Enlightened Church (1:18)
Ephesians Chapter 2 - It is an Embracing Church (2:19)
Ephesians Chapter 3 - It is an Engaging Church (3:10)
Ephesians Chapter 4 - It is an Equipping Church (4:12)
Ephesians Chapter 5 - It is an Exemplary Church (5:1)
Ephesians Chapter 6 - It is an Enduring Church (6:11)

A Church that has found real purpose in its existence on earth will be passionate in its priorities. It will never lack enthusiasm and engagement since the church is an agent of transformation of lives and societies. If the community is privileged to have a purpose -driven, mission-oriented, and Spirit-empowered Church, the   Kingdom peace and presence is evident in its neighbourhoods. Restoration of the Purpose of the Church is the key to restoring lost values and saving lives in our world.

28. A RESTORED MIND
(Philippians 2:5)

Can you imagine a person without the benefit of the function of mind? The mind is a powerful gift and endowment in human creation. Man is distinct in God's creation, in that he has been equipped with the ability to think, reason and make decisions and choices in life. Though God created man with a healthy mind, body, soul and spirit the entrance of sin and man's choice of disobeying God's Word has caused the mind to be darkened and corrupted.(Ephesians 4:18; 2:1-3; 2 Corinthians 3:14; Romans 1:21).

Human mind is desperately in need of repair, renewal and restoration. The Apostle Paul wrote, " ...and be renewed in the spirit of your mind..." (Ephesians 4:23).Paul's primary theme and emphasis in the Letter to the Philippians is that, only in Christ are real unity and joy possible. In this epistle Paul focuses on the Christ like mind, and encourages all believers to put on this attitude to keep the unity in the body of Christ.

Let us discover four essential qualities of a restored and healthy mind:

1. **A Single Mind** (Philippians 1:27)- ".. that you stand fast in one spirit, with one mind striving together for the faith of the gospel". Paul must have heard reports of or identified a spirit of disunity in the Church in Philippi. He knows well the power of united efforts for the furtherance of the gospel. Also the schemes of the enemy to divide and distance believers with petty issues could hinder the progress and advancement of the work of God. Therefore he writes emphatically to have the singleness of mind and to strive together for the faith of the gospel. Divided minds can destroy the church and its influence in the community. May the Lord unite us and give us a single mind.

2.**A Servant Mind** (Philippians 2:5-7)- "Let this mind be in you, which was also in Christ Jesus, taking the form of a bond servant..." A person may be "a mindless servant" or "servant minded" in his/her disposition. True service is sacrificial, self-less, and sincere, without expecting anything in return or a reward /recognition. A servant serves, because his mind is tuned and fashioned to be a servant in season and out of season. Christ is the supreme example for servant mindedness. He taught us that humility makes us to be great. (Matthew 20:26; 23:11,12).

3. **A Spiritual Mind** (Philippians 3:3)- A person who is not born again and transformed by the gospel and the Spirit of God possesses a carnal, fleshly, corrupted mind that has no regard for Godly things. Paul reminds the believers in Philippi that their identity is not in the law or any traditions that they were brought up. Instead he wrote that they worship God in the Spirit. True worship is offered with our whole being- body, soul, spirit, mind, emotions, and feelings. A carnal mind cannot offer spiritual worship. A renewed and restored mind is a spiritual mind that is created to serve God. Our spiritual mind is set on things above. (Colossians 3:1-2).

4. **A Secure Mind** (Philippians 4:6-7)-When your mind is filled with anxious, negative, unwholesome and destructive thoughts you are not at ease. Your inner peace is gone out and restlessness settle in! We hear at times people say , "It's all in the mind". a restored mind is a restful mind, always at peace knowing he/she is filled with the peace of God. " ..and the peace of God, which surpasses all understanding, will guard your hearts and minds through Christ Jesus."

29. RESTORE, OR BE REMOVED!

The God of the Bible is a loving, caring, forgiving and merciful Saviour, Who patiently waits for all those who have forsaken Him to return and be restored. "His mercy endures for ever" says the Psalmist in Psalm 136.The merciful God is also a righteous and just father who expects His chosen ones to be in obedience and submission to His voice.

The messages to the Seven Churches in the Book of Revelation has commendations and corrections. Those churches are representatives of the churches of all generations. We may learn important principles and practical applications for our time.

Let us learn the following from the church in Ephesus:

1. **It was a Remarkable Church** (Revelation 2:2-3)- It was an outstanding church with an incredible track record. The Lord knew and recognised the serious and sanctified nature of this body of people in the city of Ephesus. There were distinct qualities that sustained the Church in the midst of trials, compromise and other challenges. This Church made its head (Christ) feel proud of it. May we learn to be a church as this in being a true Body of Christ with an excellent spirit and disposition? Let each Christian be a person of character and calibre to stand firm and remain faithful and be commended by our Master.

2. **It became a Relapsed Church** (Revelation 2:4)- Jesus said this about the Ephesian Church, "Nevertheless, I have this against you, that you have left your first love." To be relapsed means, reverted, deteriorated, degenerated, worsened, lapsed to go back to and to fall back. All the distinct qualities and privileges they possessed were gone when they chose to leave the first love they had to the Lord. "You have left your first love" says Jesus. It was not an accident, but a deliberate and conscious act whereby the church chose to leave the priority and major on the minors. It is dangerous for a church to leave the link and love from the head (Christ).

3. **It had serious Reminders from the Lord** (Revelation 2:5)

•   **Remember-** The Lord wants the Church in Ephesus to go back and remember where they were and where they are now! This is often a first step towards full restoration. Turn back and see and be reminded of the first love between the Lord Jesus and the Church! Brother, sister do you love Jesus now as you first loved Him?

•   **Repent-** Be sorry for and turn back from wrongful/sinful paths and turn towards and walk with Christ- this is true repentance. The Church of today must repent and be restored. Every believer is asked to repent and receive God's pardon each day. Every known and unknown sins must be confessed and forgiven by Christ.

•   **Remove-** " .. or else I will come to you quickly and remove your lamp stand from its place unless you repent" says Jesus to the Ephesian Church. A loveless church is a waste of time and space. When the church in Ephesus ceased to be the light bearer on its lamp stand, the Lord of the Church will have to make a serious decision- to remove it from its place. A barren tree will be cut off, salt that lost its flavour will be thrown out to be trampled over, and a loveless, light-less church also will be removed.

30. RESTORING OUR CHILDREN

We hear from parents, guardians and generally from other concerned family members that how difficult it is to bring up our children in this perverted and crooked generation. Even the parents and guardians who are seriously making an effort to discipline and raise up the children to be morally pure and ethically fair and just are often restricted an frustrated by all kinds of influences and forces, both external and internal.

Let us remember the following as we deal with this serious matter:

1. **Discipline for Children is desired (Proverbs 22:6, 15)**

"A youngster's heart is filled with foolishness, but physical discipline will drive it far away"(NLT). Wise King Solomon has given us many warnings and exhortations in this matter. A denial, delay and difference from the biblical instructions on the discipline and nurturing of children could result in a different destiny and even in disaster! Let us discipline while there is time and bring up our children in Christ like character. (Hebrews 12:5-11)

2. **Instruction and Training in the Word is essential (2 Timothy 3:14-17)**

Paul the apostle took time to instruct and train young Timothy to be shaped as a man of God. The Bible is our text book, the parents, teachers and instructors are the tools which God uses to develop the character of Christ and the Biblical moral values in our children. May we prepare ourselves to offer sound teachings and moral values that will be engraved in the hearts of our children and youth.

3. **Children look for role models to follow (2 Timothy 3:10)**

Paul wrote to Timothy, "But you have carefully followed my doctrine, manner of life....." Kids are copycats! We hear children saying at times, "When I grow up, I want to be like ....". They dream about becoming like super stars, celebrities, and experts and so on in this world. But how many of our children will say, they want to serve God and influence their world for Jesus? However, if they have wrong influence and negative role models that are harmful to life and society our children will never become change agents for the good. The Scripture says, " Evil company corrupts good habits" (1 Corinthians 15: 33). Let us guide our children in what they watch on TV, internet, YouTube, let's see who they move with and what they read and what are their passions. If we find any areas of concern and doubts, sit with them and clarify and explain and warn any dangerous spots that could badly influence them. Above all we as parents and church folks may we each be good role models for our children to follow.

31. RESTORATION PROMISES OF God
Jeremiah 29:10-14

The God of the Bible is a Father Who is willing to extend His love and mercy to the fallen, failed and frustrated children. He cannot deny Himself of His nature and character. He has proven throughout the history of God's people that He is a God of restoration. His promises are always trustworthy and we can count on Him to fulfil the promises.

Jeremiah, the prophet has predicted the promises of God to the people of Israel during their captivity years- Seventy Years in Babylon. Let us list a few of them as we see in the Scriptures. God said,

1. **I Will Visit You** (Jeremiah 28:10)- This is God's extension of his love and compassion. Instead of abandoning the rebellious people altogether, the Father-hearted God declares that " I will visit you". Yes indeed history proves that God has visited the Israelites many times and rescued them.

2. **I Think Towards You** (Jeremiah 28:11)-God as the Father could not rest until His distanced children are settled in their rightful place. Israel was always in the mind of God. He had thoughts of peace and offers of a great future and hope for them.

3. **I Will Listen to You** (Jeremiah 28:12)- Who will listen to a group of people who have turned against and refused to comply with? Israel has grieved God time and again, and rejected His voice and commandments and walked in their own futile minds. But look what a promise God has offered to them, " I will listen to you" when you pray.

4. **I Will Bring You Back** (Jeremiah 28:14)- This is the best promise Israel can ever receive from their God and Father. A promise of return, and relocation. In captivity in the foreign land, they were without the Temple and all the authentic articles required for worship. They do not have to stay in the captivity too long. Restoration has come. It is home time.

5. **I Will Gather You** (Jeremiah 28:14)- Scattered must be gathered, lost must be found, distanced must be brought nearer, rejected must be welcomed, for restoration to be complete. The restorer is not any human parent or an institution. Then there will be conditions, restrictions, stipulations and limitations. But when God gathers His run-away, rebellious children no man can hinder.

6. **I Will Bring You to the Place** (Jeremiah 28:14)- Restoration is not fully satisfactory until the item, person, spiritual quality etc has been brought back to its original and superior quality. From Israel they went out as captives, and to Israel they will be brought back as citizens. From the city of Jerusalem with its glory and beauty they left, but to the city itself they will be brought to resettle. The place (Jerusalem) is so important to the Jew that they are not "at home" if they are far from the temple, worship, Law and other observances and practices of their faith.

The God of Israel is the God of all flesh! He has a message of restoration for you. He will restore you from your failures, frustration, fears, low self esteem, anxieties, concerns and worries He is faithful in His promises. Just trust Him. Your time of restoration is coming. Wait for the Lord. You will never be ashamed.

32. RESTORING THE FALLEN

The ministry of restoring the fallen among the believers is not often given a priority in the community of faith. Very many churches and groups are too busy and pre occupied with church work and this mission of rescue, repair and restoration is neglected. Christ and the early Christian Church had a focus on reaching out and bringing such wounded and wandering brethren and restoring them.

Who are the "fallen" and in need of restoration?

1. Those who are Fallen in Sin (Galatians 6:1)- Please see the various translations of the verse, "If someone falls into in.."(Message); "if a person gets trapped by wrong thing.."(God's Word); " if a man is overtaken (caught) in any trespass" (NKJV); "if a Christian overcome by some sin..."(LB). Notice, this is a believer in Christ and a member of the Body of Christ who is fallen from his/her position, privilege and progress in the faith.

These brethren have fallen in their practical, ethical, moral life style; instead of following Christ's example they had conformed to this world (Romans 12:2). Mistakes and failures can happen to the saintliest person, but he/she does not have to remain in the fallen state. The God of Restoration has made a way for such to be brought back and re-established in the Church. We are told to "forgivingly and in a spirit of gentleness torestore" such ones. Let the Church take this challenge seriously and bring back the fallen and entrapped believers.

2. Those who Wanders from the Truth (James 5:19)- The truth for all to follow and practice has been revealed and recorded in the Holy Scriptures. In the passing of time and change of season and cultures and by the pressure of false teachers the truth has been compromised and diluted. Many have wandered off from the truth and adopted teachings and life styles that are convenient to them and suit their own comforts and cultures. However, truth remains truth even in the midst of all changes and seasons.

Wandering off from truth can be deliberate, under manipulation, and due to enticements and pressures from the enemies of the true teachings of the Scriptures. "They slip away from God and no longer trusts the Lord" (LB). "Wandered off from God's truth, don't write them off" (The Message). Someone can bring that person back and make him understand the Truth again. The Church must take the ministry of discipleship seriously, and establish each new believer, and ground them in the fundamentals and foundations of the Christian faith.

3. Those who have Forsaken the Family of God (2 Timothy 4:11)- Paul the Apostle wrote from the prison as he felt a little lonely and left out by many in his last days. He wrote to Timothy, "Get mark and bring him with you, for he is useful to me for ministry". Mark was an assistant in Paul's first missionary trip (Acts 13:5), but when they reached Perga in Pamphylia, John Mark left the company and returned to Jerusalem. He abandoned the group and forsaken the task of assisting in the mission work. Paul wrote about Demas who also forsaken him having loved this present world (2 Timothy 4:10). Restoration of the Fallen, Frustrated, Faint -hearted, Forsaken, and Feeble brethren must be looked into seriously. God's grace is sufficient to bring back the Fallen, Wandering and Forsaken ones.

33. PROMISE, PRESCRIPTION AND PRAYER FOR RESTORATION

The Book of Lamentations is an eyewitness record of the destruction of Jerusalem and its people by the King of Babylon. Nebuchadnezzar and his army invaded the holy city around B.C. 600, plundering the city of its gold and treasures and exiling its people to Babylon. Israel, as the chosen people of God are displaced and are without temple worship and the festivals and ceremonies that were closer to their hearts. They are longing for a restoration!

Jeremiah's lamentations are representative of all those who sincerely feel the loss of their identity and privileges in God. The Book of Lamentations is filled with a condition of misery, depression and hopelessness. But in the midst of all the sadness, tears and hopelessness the God of Israel promises a restoration and has suggested the prescription and encourages prayers for genuine restoration.

1. **The Promise of Restoration** (Lamentations 3:31-33)- The people of Israel were in a desperate situation as they were captured and transported to a foreign country. The chosen people with a divine destiny are now in a strange land. It is their rebellion, stubbornness and disobedience to the commands of Jehovah that brought them to such a situation. However, God has not forgotten His covenant with Abraham and his descendents and is offering them promises of restoration: "For the Lord will not cast off forever. Though He causes grief, yet he will show compassion, according to the multitude of His mercies. For He does not afflict willingly nor grieve the children of men." God cannot abandon His treasure and His chosen people. His promises are for you, no matter where you are or what condition you are in now. You can trust the promises of our God.

2. **The Prescription for Restoration** (Lamentations 2:19)- The prescription from a physician is beneficial for the health and well being of our body. Our spiritual sickness also requires a spiritual remedy and prescription. The children of Israel were broken in their spirits and " their heart cried out to the Lord" (Lamentations2:18) They began to shed tears, and gave no rest to their eyes. They began to cry out in the night, pouring their hearts like water before the face of the Lord. When was the last time you cried out in desperation to the Lord in a critical condition? Have you sought the Lord seriously and sincerely and searched the Scriptures for guidance and support in times of depression, desertion, distance and divisions in the family, church and in the community? Let us cry out and pour our hearts before God.

3. **The Prayer for Restoration** (Lamentations 5:19-22)- The promise and prescription is brought to actual fulfilment by the passionate prayer of the people who needs restoration. The prophet Jeremiah had prayed on behalf of all the displaced Israelites, "Turn us back to You, O Lord and we will be restored. Renew our days as of old."(Lamentations 5:21).The God of the Bible is a covenant God who keeps His promise and acts on behalf of His people. As long as the Israelites are staying away from the land of their fathers, God cannot fulfil His Word. The distanced people must be brought nearer and resettle in the Promised Land. "Turn us back to You" is the prayer. Before we can be restored to the place, position and privilege God has prepared, we must return to Him personally. Is it your prayer to be restored to God first? Psalm 80:3, "Restore us O God; cause Your face to shine, and we shall be saved." Let us pray like the Psalmist and the prophet.

34. DAVID'S RECOVERY
"David recovered all" (1 Samuel 30:18, 19)

The experiences and events in the life of King David are described in the books of First and Second Samuel. He was known as the "man after God's own heart," though there were sin stains in his life. David's life was full of ups and downs, but God's covenant with him and the Messianic predictions through him required a restoration and a renewal.

There was a time in David's life, when he suffered great loss and had to go through distress and despair (1 Samuel 30:4-6). The enemies of Israel, Amalekites, had invaded the South and Ziklag and plundered goods and taken captive women and all those who were there. Among the captives were David's two wives- Ahinoam and Abigail. The loss of loved ones and possessions were so much that the "soul of all the people was grieved." It was felt deeply in their hearts and affected terribly the courage and hope of all men. Let us observe the following steps David took in recovering all:

1. **David Strengthened himself in the Lord** (1 Samuel 30:6)- The loss of people and properties could naturally eat up our stamina and courage. A weakness in our minds and spirits settle in when we feel the loss and mourn over the missing ones. When you look around and cannot find any comfort, there is strength in the Lord. "David strengthened himself in the Lord." The Source and supply is the Lord. Recovery begins by resting in the Lord.

2. **David Inquired of the Lord** (1 Samuel 30:8)- This is a crucial step : that is asking God, before David himself does anything towards recovering the lost people and property. Seeking first God's guidance and support in all matters is a pattern for all believers to follow. (Matthew 6:33). His trust in the Lord and the knowledge of God's character prompted David to inquire of the Lord.

3. **David Pursued** (1 Samuel 30:10)- Here is action from David to recover that which was lost and taken away from him. This is to do with following and chasing the enemy in the strength and under the guidance of the Lord. Along with the exercise of our faith and courage, we are called to move forward and take back that which belongs to us forcefully from the hands of the enemy. David went with a   company of six hundred men to rescue that which was taken away. Resist the devil and he will flee.

4. **David Recovered all** (1 Samuel 30:18)- "So David recovered all that the Amalekites had carried away, and David rescued his two wives." Restoration is not complete until that which is missing is brought back home and replaced. We feel the loss and a vacuum if the essential components for peace and stability are missing from our lives. What are certain core values and foundational principles that make you a believer who is truly content? Recovering few items and some people will not be a complete rescue or recovery. "David recovered all," says the Scriptures.

Let us take some time and see where we have lost as far as spirituality and Christ likeness is concerned? May we examine ourselves and discover the neglects and abandonment of Godly living, first love and sacrificial service to humanity and the Kingdom of God. David recovered all, and so must you.

35. RESTORATION OF REAL LOVE

Jesus said, "Greater love has no one than this, than to lay down one's life for his friends" (John 15:13). We hear a lot of people making statements as these: "love is God", "love is the greatest thing", "it doesn't matter as long as love is there." Sadly all these are not true statements, though they sound good and appealing to many people. The truth of the matter is that the God of the Bible is a God of love. "God is love", says John the Apostle. What is man's response to God's love? Let us examine Five of them as follows:

1. **It is a Leaning Love** (John 13:23)- The disciple whom Jesus loved was leaning on His bosom. While Jesus was approaching His crucifixion, He gathered the Twelve disciples and told them that one of them would betray Him. Therefore, hearing this, all of them were questioning each other and asking who this person could be. But the disciple who was consumed with the love of Jesus was seated closer to Him and seems undisturbed with the questions of colleagues. Leaning on Jesus' bosom shows that the love of the disciple was content, settled, undisturbed, and free from anxiety.

2. **It is a Lingering Love** (John19:26)- Here we see Jesus is on the cross, hanging, bleeding, thirsty, agonising, praying, forgiving and about to die. A very scary place and disturbing time for many people. All His disciples had fled, not one to be seen around, except the one who calls himself "the disciple whom Jesus loved". He is standing beside the cross along with Jesus' mother and other women. Real love lingers, when all others leave. This love holds on, stays beside, not abandoned in crisis. "Who shall separate us from the love of Christ?" (Romans 8:35).

3. **It is a Longing Love** (John 20:2-5)- Jesus, after being crucified and buried has risen from the grave. The women who went to anoint the body of Jesus, early in the morning after the Sabbath found the tomb empty. They reported to Peter and other disciples that the body of Jesus must have been taken away. Immediately Peter and the disciple whom Jesus loved ran to the tomb, the beloved one outran Peter and reached the tomb first. It is the genuineness of his love and the longing to see the body of Jesus that drove him to the tomb. Are you driven by the unconditional love that longs to see the Lord?

4. **It is a Listening Love** (John 21:7)- "Therefore, the disciple whom Jesus loved said to Peter, It is the Lord!".The risen Lord Jesus has been appearing to his 11 disciples and others in various places and times. At one occasion, while the company of disciples were fishing, and failed in their efforts and caught nothing. Jesus appeared to them and spoke to them and offered them a fishing suggestion. But they did not recognise Him, except the beloved disciple. He recognised the voice of the Master and responded to the rest and said, "It is the Lord!" The real love has listening ears and a spirit of understanding. Do you hear the Master's voice in the Word, in your prayers, worship, meditation, and in your crisis?

5. **It is a Liberated Love** (John 21:20)- "Then...saw the disciple whom Jesus loved following.." Peter lost the passion and vision for a little while after Jesus' crucifixion and death and went for fishing. Jesus had to reinstate him, making him to confess three times to say, " I love you". A confrontation before consecration and commissioning for future task in the mission of the Master. Let our love be without hypocrisy. If you have left your first love, it is time to restore, renew and revive. The Master is looking for those who love Him and serve Him sincerely.

36. RESTORATION OF REVIVAL

"Will you not revive us again, that your people may rejoice in you?" (Psalm 85:6)
"Revival" is a word that has been used in the Christian circles many times over
the centuries. It is a term that portrays new life, recovery, revitalization, renewal,
vibrancy, liveliness, stimulation, productivity, effectiveness and a freshness in the
lives and services of people and community. Do we need a revival today? Let us
examine the Scriptures and make the way clear for a restoration of revival times.

1. **What is Revival?**- Let us look at few definitions of "Revival" from the experts who
have experienced and have done research in the field of spiritual renewal.

"Revival is a community saturated with God."- Duncan Campbell

" A revival is nothing else than a new beginning of obedience to God."- Charles Finney

True revival is not man- made, or orchestrated by a church or a missions agency. It is
the sovereign and mighty move of the Spirit of God whereby people and communities
and nations are changed by the power and presence of God.

2. **The Need for Revival!**- "When is a revival needed? When carelessness and
unconcern keep the people asleep." said Billy Sunday. The dead cannot be revived,
they need resurrection! Only the living and those that are about to die, or are losing
their power and usefulness need a mighty revival.

In the Book of Revelation (Chapters 2 and 3) the Apostle John has mentioned the
following churches that are desperately in need of a revival: Ephesus (the loveless
Church); Thyatira (The corrupt Church); Sardis (the dead Church); Laodicea (the
lukewarm Church). The Church of today in general has lost the credibility in the
community where it exists. The salt has lost its saltiness and became ineffective. The
light has become so dim that the path way is not visible and the neighborhood is in
darkness. We need a revival NOW!

3. **The Price of Revival**- The history of revival clearly speaks of a price that had been
paid by the faithful ones, for the revival to come and saturate communities and
quicken people. The first revival of the New Testament (Acts Chapter 2) itself had
a committed group of Christ-followers in constant prayer before the Pentecost was
manifested. The Welsh Revival of 1904 was preceded by fervent prayer, confession,
repentance and restitution by a group of awakened youth under the leadership of Evan
Roberts. God is still faithful to honour His Word and fulfil His promise to His people.

" If My people who are called by My Name will humble themselves, and pray and
seek My face, and turn from their wicked ways, then I will hear from heaven, and
will forgive their sin and heal their land." says the Lord (2 Chronicles 7:14). Who is
willing to pay the price today? Evan Roberts and his fellow prayer warriors prayed
and repented "Bend the Church and save the people"! Who will stand in the gap and
intercede? (Ezekiel 22:30).

Revival is the need of the hour. God will send a revival in answer to the preparation of
His people. Are we ready to pay the price and reap a harvest? Let the Holy Spirit sent
revival come.

37. MISSION OF THE CHURCH

Jesus Said," As the Father has sent Me, I also send you." (John 20:21) We are all familiar with the terms, "mission", "missionary" or "missions" in the Christian circles. The general meaning of "mission" is assignment, task, undertaking, charge, duty etc. The Church of God was instituted by Christ on earth to accomplish the Great Commission of the Lord (Matthew 28:19, 20).

For the last nearly two thousand years the Church is sent out into the world to preach the Good News of the Gospel, to make disciples of all nations, and prepare the believers to be active members of the Body of Christ till the Kingdom of God comes in its fullness. The Four Gospels, the Acts of the Apostles and the Letters of the New Testament and the Book of Revelation testifies and affirms the mission of the Church.

We need a restoration in our Mission because of:

1. **The Omission of the Mission**- The Great Commission of Christ has become the "great omission" in the Christian Church generally. In other words, the priority of preaching, teaching, baptizing, making disciples, reaching the unreached people groups and building healthy growing churches are no longer emphasized. Instead welfare projects, educational, cultural, community development programmes are promoted and it has come to an end in itself.

2. **The Mission without Vision** (Matthew 9:36-38; John 4:35)- Jesus is the greatest Visionary and the most excellent Missionary ever. His mission was with a vision of the people who needed desperately the Good News and its benefits to the total man. Isaiah, the prophet received a transforming vision of the Lord, of himself and the unclean people around him before he was commissioned. (Isaiah 6:1-9). You cannot reap that which you do not see! Seeing the lost condition of the human soul and that there is no other way (Name) for man's redemption, should bring a renewal in our mission.

3. **The Mission without Passion** (Lamentations 3:51)- "Jeremiah the prophet wept and wrote, "My eyes bring suffering to my soul, because of the daughters of my city". "Passion" is the craving, the urge and the deep motivation generated by vision to accomplish something that requires urgent attention from us. The lost and unreached people in the world are many millions and they all will end up in a destiny without Christ! Are those churches that have undertaken some mission projects and sent missionaries, do the work seriously and passionately?

4. **The Mission without Provision**- Every mission and task requires man power, resources and finances. The Apostle Paul commends the Church in Philippi for their partnership and provisions in his ministry. They sent man power and finances to support Paul's ministry (Phil. 4:15-18).When the Church undertakes the mission of reaching the unreached it must consider providing and maximising the resources the mission requires.

5. **The Mission without Supervision**- An un supervised, and ill equipped mission engagement leads to confusion. The pattern of the New Testament missions as we read in the Book of Acts and the Letters of Paul are filled with principles for successful and practical launching and sustaining of the work of the Church. The Church is the sending agency under the guidance of the Holy Spirit (Acts 13:1-4). The Church is the receiving/host agency for the missionaries who returned and reported their work (Acts 14:26-28)

Does your Church's mission needs restoration and renewal? A Church with a restored mission and renewed vision will be driven by a passion and will sustain the mission of Christ till He comes. Amen.

38. Restoring Hope

"Hope differed makes the heart sick, but when dreams come true, there is life and joy" (Proverbs 13:12) "Abraham, contrary to hope, in hope believed..." (Romans 4:18)

"Hope" is defined as confidence, expectation, anticipation, optimism, courage, faith etc. It is an essential ingredient in the making of a healthy and positive human life. Despair is the opposite of hope and is destructive if prolonged in people and environment. When God created man he was in the best of spirit and health and in an environment that has nurtured hope, peace and life.

Today, hope is a rare experience and seldom expected in the lives of people everywhere. The divine investment of positive trust and hopefulness is missing in man and a sense of fear and despair has settled in the hearts of people. Sin and rebellion, distancing from the life of God, and relying on self are reasons for the loss of this precious ingredient in man. Can the lost hope be restored? Is there hope in times like fear, threats, danger, and famine, loss of things, jobs, loved ones and even our health? Yes hope differed can be restored.

Restoration of hope is brought by the following steps:

1. **Remembrance of the Presence of God** (Psalm 42:4)- The sons of Korah wrote this psalm as they contemplated on the privileges and provisions of God in the midst of distresses. When your soul is restless and hope and peace is nowhere to be found, it is time to remind yourself of the source of life and hope. The enemy will question you "Where is your God?" and you need to refresh your memories of God's presence and your previous praises and joyful experiences in Him. Isn't it time you engage in renewed praises and expressions of thanksgiving in anticipation, because our God is ever-present and never failing? "Hope in God; for I shall yet praise Him.." (Psalm 42:11)

2. **Reassurance of the Promises of God** (Haggai 2:5-9)- Prophet Haggai was sent to a community of dispirited people, who had given up on their spiritual progress and development and turned to selfish agendas and became losers of hope and joy. These Jewish returnees from Babylonian captivity had a mandate to complete the construction of the temple of God in Jerusalem. But it seems the enthusiasm is lost and their hope is short lived. Now God has spoken to them through the prophet, and re assured them of His promise of : His presence, plans for the future, the popularity of the project they have undertaken, and His peace. God's promises give us hope in hopelessness and in every crisis. "Abraham, contrary to hope, in hope believed" (Romans 4:18). Be assured that God keeps His promises and you can trust Him.

3. **Remain in the Plan of God** (Jeremiah 29:11)- At times we may not fully understand the plans and purposes God has for each of us. Especially, when we are faced with critical experiences and unfavourable conditions in life, we seem to lose all hope. But God's plan is always ultimately for our good and His glory. The Israelites who were taken by

Babylonians were desperately dreaming of returning to their home land. But God said," I will visit you and perform My good word toward you, after seventy years are completed in Babylon.." (Jere.29:10). So long as you remain and rest in the divine plan, your hope will be restored.

God said, " I know the thoughts that I think toward you,.. thoughts of peace and not of evil, to give you a future and a hope" (Jere. 29:11). God's plan is always a plan for future and restoration of hope.

God can restore your hope and make you a person of praise, purpose and peace as you take these and further steps in your life.

May you be restored in peace and hope.

◊♦♦♦■■♦♦◊